Imperialism and Internationalism

Socialist History 13

Edited by
Willie Thompson,
David Parker, Mike Waite,
David Morgan and
Heather Williams

Rivers Oram Press
London and New York

Editorial Team
Willie Thompson
David Parker
Rodney Hilton
Mike Waite
David Morgan
Heather Williams

Editorial Advisors
Noreen Branson
Eric Hobsbawm
David Howell
Monty Johnstone
Victor Kiernan
David Marquand
Kevin Morgan
Ben Pimlott
Pat Thane

Published in 1998
by Rivers Oram Press
144 Hemingford Road, London N1 1DE

Distributed in the USA by
New York University Press
Elmer Holmes Bobst Library
70 Washington Square South
New York, NY 10012-1091

Set in Garamond by
NJ Design Associates, Romsey, Hants
and printed in Great Britain by
T.J. International Ltd, Padstow, Cornwall

This edition copyright © Socialist History Society 1998

No part of this journal may be produced in any form, except for the quotation of brief passages in criticism, without the written permission of the publishers. The right of the contributors to be identified as the authors has been asserted by them in accordance with the Copyright, Designs and Patents Act 1988

British Library Cataloguing in Publication Data
A catalogue record for this publication is available from the British Library
ISBN 1 85489 106 5 (hb)
ISBN 1 85489 107 3 (pb)
ISSN 0969 4331

Contents

Editorial

Empires and Umpires 1
Victor Kiernan

Indian Nationalism: Before and After Independence 23
Ralph Russell

Aliens and Little Britons 37
Anna Davin

An Illegal Immigrant in South Africa 53
Bill McCaig

Delegation to Kurdistan 57
David Morgan

Reviews
Great Power Complex — British Imperialism, International Crises and National Decline edited by John Callaghan
Kenneth Lunn 60

A Medieval Mercantile Community — The Grocers' Company and the Politics and Trade of London 1000–1485 by Pamela Nightingale
Heather Swanton 62

Che Guevara: A Revolutionary Life by John Lee Anderson
Maria Black 65

Democratisation in Eastern Europe edited by Geoffrey Pridham and Tatu Vanhanen
Eastern Europe in the Twentieth Century by R.J. Crampton
Martin Myant   **69**

Das War Unser Leben: Erinnerungen und Dockumente zur der Freien Deutschen Jügend in Grossbritannien 1939–1946 edited by Alfred Fleischacker
Marian Fagan   **72**

Labour and Society in Britain and the USA by Neville Kirk
John Saville   **74**

Wollstonecraft's Daughters: Womanhood in England and France, 1780–1920 edited by Clarissa Campbell Orr
Christine Collette   **77**

The Great Alliance: Economic Recovery and the Problems of Power, 1945–1951 by Jim Phillips
Nina Fishman   **80**

Shop Floor Citizens: Engineering Democracy in 1940s Britain by James Hinton
Jim Fyrth   **84**

Class and Politics in a Northern Industrial Town: Keighley 1880–1914 by David James
Malcolm Starrs   **89**

A History of Conservative Politics 1900–1996 by John Charmley
From Salisbury to Major: Continuity and Change in Conservative Politics by Brendan Evans and Andrew Taylor
Andrew Gamble   **93**

Books Received   **96**
Correspondence   **98**

Index   **99**

Editorial

Readers will note that with No. 13 *Socialist History* has been given a new look. The redesign of our cover and other changes — as well as delayed publication of the first issue of 1998 — follows on from the change of our publisher from Pluto Press to Rivers Oram. The association with Pluto over five years enabled us to establish from the combination of *Socialist History Journal* and *Our History*, our former publications, a viable historical journal with serious high-quality content and professional appearance, well-regarded among historians in the left-wing tradition and more widely. We fully expect that this new development will be accompanied with even further advances in the range of our contributors and the diffusion of the journal. We are confident too that an opportunity has been created to attract new readers, and we extend a welcome to any of those joining the journal at this point.

Contents of No. 13

Imperialism has featured among the central realities of the past century (and earlier) and did not disappear with the formal dissolution of colonial empires in the decades following the Second World War. Its impact can be measured both in what it did and continues to do, the societies upon which it was inflicted and the consequences which followed for the states which perpetrated it.

At the same time it was the age of empire which brought to the world a hitherto inconceivable measure of economic unity, predecessor of the globalisation of our own age; covering the globe with a network of railway systems, steamship routes and telegraph wires; instituting a world currency for international trade in the shape of the pound sterling. It was in the same era, and partly in reaction to imperialism's development, that the concept of internationalism also made its appearance in an institutional form. The Socialist International, founded in 1889, was the first political organisation to transcend national boundaries and to call upon the working classes of various nations to co-operate against their rulers in a programme of social emancipation. That internationalism however proved to be a frail plant, soon blighted in the climate of imperial rivalries which came to dominate the opening years of the twentieth century and culminated in the First World War.

In the world economic crisis of the succeeding years, still more morbid varieties of imperialism appeared and briefly flourished in the shape of the fascist dictatorships, while internationalism and anti-colonialism came above all to be represented by the Communist International and the parties which adhered to it. The inherent instability and aggressiveness of the fascist regimes soon brought about their destruction; the liquidation of European political sovereignty over dependent territories in Asia and Africa (and the Caribbean) followed in a historically very short span of time. Imperialism in the old style was replaced in our era by economic domination exercised through the mechanisms of the global market.

Victor Kiernan opens the present issue of *Socialist History* by tracing this process of development, and at the same time he considers some of the leading interpretations of imperialism's meaning and significance, both Marxist and otherwise, which have dominated the field. Following this survey we offer items which examine different specific aspects of the history of imperialism and internationalism. Ralph Russell provides an insight into the enormously complicated developments which led up to the independence of India and Pakistan following the partition of the British Raj, in which the main participants were the British government, the Indian National Congress and the Muslim League, all pushed by the pressures of incipient mass revolt.

Anna Davin addresses a wholly different angle of imperialism's heritage. Among the strongest ideological props of empire was the inculcation of assumptions among the general British public of innate superiority over foreigners and over the 'native' peoples spread across the globe and governed from Westminster and Whitehall. Her article examines the situation of early twentieth-century London as an imperial capital governed by imperial culture and assumptions assimilating or failing to assimilate a constant stream of immigrants of diverse ethnic backgrounds and subject to frequent misunderstanding and racial prejudice.

But if racism has constituted a broad and ugly current within British culture, it has at the same time been combated by anti-racist and anti-imperialist forces. An example of involvement in anti-imperialist solidarity on behalf of the liberation movement in South Africa during the apartheid era is recounted by Bill McCaig. David Morgan reports on a recent visit he undertook to Turkish Kurdistan in solidarity with the persecuted inhabitants of that region.

A selection of reviews complete this number of *Socialist History*, some of them directly linked to the main theme, and others of a more varied scope. No. 14, under the thematic title 'The Future of History' will focus on various dimensions of historical methodology and include the proceedings of a round table of eminent historians.

Finally — an apology to all our patient reviewers whose reviews have been held up on account of the limited space available to us — we expect to clear the backlog over the course of this number and No. 14.

The Editors

Socialist History Journal

The *Socialist History Journal* explores and assesses the past of the socialist movement and broader processes in relation to it, not only for the sake of historical understanding, but as an input and contribution to the movement's future development. The journal is not exclusive and welcomes argument and debate from all viewpoints.

Other *Socialist History* titles:

A Bourgeois Revolution?
Socialist History 1 · 1993
0 7453 08058

What Was Communism? Pt 1
Socialist History 2 · 1993
0 7453 08066

What Was Communism? Pt 2
Socialist History 3 · 1993
0 7453 08074

The Labour Party Since 1945
Socialist History 4 · 1994
0 7453 08082

The Left and Culture
Socialist History 5 · 1994
0 7453 08090

The Personal and the Political
Socialist History 6 · 1994
0 7453 08104

Fighting the Good Fight?
Socialist History 7 · 1995
0 7453 10613

Historiography and the British Marxist Historians
Socialist History 8 · 1995
0 7453 08120

Labour Movements
Socialist History 9 · 1996
0 7453 08139

Revisions?
Socialist History 10 · 1996
0 7453 08147

The Cold War
Socialist History 11 · 1997
0 7453 12411

Nationalism and Communist Party History
Socialist History 12 · 1997
0 7453 12675

Imperialism and Internationalism
Socialist History 13 · 1998
1 85489 1073

The Future of History
Socialist History 14 · 1998
1 85489 1154

Empires and Umpires
Victor Kiernan

How Sarawak became British

The 1850s was a decade of excitements as Europe emerged dizzily from the revolutionary upheaval of 1848–9 and sought reassurance in successes far away. The Crimean War was fought in 1854–6 on the margins of Europe and Asia; then the tide rolled eastwards with an Anglo-Persian war in 1856–7, the Indian Mutiny in 1857–8, the Anglo-French attack on China, or the Second Opium War, ending in 1860. Jungle-covered Borneo lay somewhere halfway along the southern fringes of Asia, not far from the key route through the Malacca Straits, and might well draw the attention of a whole cluster of nations.

It had a scattering of petty rulers or chiefs, and on the north coast the Sultan of Brunei, whose successor today is reputedly the richest man in the world, thanks to his oil. A few miles from the nearby shore was the island of Labuan, with coal and a good harbour for merchants; it was obtained by the British in 1846. James Brooke, born in Benares and late of the East India Company army, got an unofficial British finger in the pie when he visited Sarawak (*Sarahwa*), the long stretch of country southward from Brunei between sea and mountains, in 1838 or 1839. Soon he was helping the Sultan to suppress a rising, and was rewarded with the governorship of the province, which he soon came to treat as his own, with himself as Raja. It had natural resources, few roads but navigable rivers, and a scanty mixed population, Sea Dayaks the most numerous, Malays and Chinese traders.[1]

Not far away Britain had bought Singapore from a Malay ruler in 1824; France took possession of Saigon and Cochin-China in 1861. America was taking an interest in trade routes to the Far East, and in 1854 Commodore Perry forced on Japan its first move towards opening its doors. Spain owned the Philippines and had hazy claims on Sabah, the northern tip of Borneo. Most closely concerned was Holland, which had acquired Java and the Spice Islands in the seventeenth century and fought naval wars with England over the lucrative spice trade. Since then Holland had sunk to a lower rank in Europe and depended heavily on its possessions in the Archipelago. In Borneo as elsewhere the Dutch were looking for new footholds, and wherever they got them competitors were shut out. Foreign Office records of the 1850s and 1860s reveal how lengthily the British government hesitated over the various courses open to it.[2] They are reminders also that foreign policy at that time was in the hands not of businessmen but of aristocrats, sometimes impatient of being prodded into tedious dogfights over unappetising bones.

A treaty had been made in 1824 with the Netherlands government, which in 1798 took over colonial authority from the two-centuries old Netherlands East India Company. Much wearisome correspondence had dragged on, and in 1852 the Under-Secretary Lord Stanley was promised a full review, to be ready as soon as he had been made 'sufficiently indignant with the other proceedings of the Netherlands government.'[3] Five years later Brooke was in serious trouble in Sarawak with a revolt of the Chinese. He managed to suppress it, and claimed that barely two thousand out of a population of four or five thousand had escaped with their lives;[4] but the affair must have reminded him of how vulnerable his situation was.

A British consul-general was posted to Brunei, Spenser St John; he was the sole official European representative there. A coal concession on Labuan had failed, but in his opinion the island might be made very valuable and ought not to be abandoned.[5] The India Office considered it worthless; the Colonial Office was more cautious. Captain Cochrane of the navy visited Brunei, but failed to meet the Sultan, who had 'unfortunately been seized by a fit.' He was a feeble ruler, Cochrane learned, who left the local chiefs to oppress his fertile country as they pleased.[6] The Admiralty believed the place to have immense potential, if only ships could be spared to put an end to piracy, that plague of the eastern seas. Lord Malmesbury, conservative Foreign Secretary, minuted his entire approval, adding 'Important.'[7] It did not stir him enough to find its way into his memoirs.

When Brooke proposed early in 1858 that Sarawak should be made a British protectorate, Malmesbury would have none of it. 'We have too many foreign possessions already.'[8] It was the businessmen of Britain who came forward to back the proposal. On 1 December *The Times* carried a report of an imposing deputation which had called on the Earl of Derby, the Tory Prime Minister, to urge the case for a protectorate. It included the Mayor of Manchester, spokesmen for other big towns, and Sir John Pender, pioneer of submarine telegraph cables. They made much of the Chinese fracas, linking it with a recent outbreak in Canton. Clearly Brooke needed protection, and if not given it he would have to throw in his hand or offer Sarawak elsewhere; both Holland and America would jump at it. Besides its rich resources, possession would make it easier for Britain to get a cable to China laid, something of great urgency.

Derby rejected the proposal firmly, declaring himself still more fully convinced by his visitors' arguments of 'the extreme inconvenience of sanctioning such undertakings as those of Sir James Brooke', good man though he personally was. It was doubtful whether he had a right to part with Sarawak to anybody. Britain already had too many dependencies, and each new one meant fresh expense. 'They were not additions of strength but of weakness.'

Others were less obdurate than Derby. The Admiralty was alarmed at the Dutch multiplying forts and stations in the interior and plainly having an eye on Sarawak; Spain was said to have occupied an island.[9] Brooke showed himself willing to hand over his fief altogether in return for compensation; a long office memorandum by the Hon. Charles Spring Rice of 7 January 1859 favoured a takeover to keep the Dutch out. The Admiralty continued staunch for a protectorate, though it admitted 'the general impolicy of establishing numerous colonies or settlements.'[10] Brooke wanted to retire, and grew querulous about all these delays. A sharp reprimand was administered in a letter drafted by the Whig Foreign Secretary Lord John Russell himself; he reminded Brooke that a British subject could not throw off his allegiance. Brooke's protest, 'I seek no favour and expect no justice,' is encircled with scathing comments in the margins.[11]

A feeling developed that things were getting out of hand and that a full investigation was called for.[12] Governor Cavanagh of Singapore took part in this; he was endeavouring to shepherd the Malay states in the direction they were eventually to take, into the British fold.[13] Lord Elgin, Viceroy of India, voted in 1863 for a protectorate, instead of a regular colony which would bring inevitable frictions and expenses. He was disturbed by the French presence in Saigon and 'the persistent endeavour of the Dutch to cripple British Trade.'[14] A policy of tacitly recognising Sarawak as an independent entity was adopted, and in 1864 a consul was stationed there; he was soon warning of Dutch, French and Spanish designs. Lord Clarendon as Foreign Secretary was in an awkward position, aware that Parliament would neither provide money for setting up a colony, nor relish seeing Sarawak as an American possession, of which there seemed a possibility.[15] The Colonial Office too feared that as a colony it would be a burden, and observed, as a piece of received wisdom, that 'commercial influence' derives not from territory but from 'ships, capital and credit.'[16]

Raja Brooke retired in 1863; the nephew who replaced him renewed in 1869 the appeal for a protectorate to be set up. He too met with a negative, after consultation with the premier Gladstone, though in more amicable language than Lord John Russell's.[17] At long last, in 1888, Britain changed its mind and took Sarawak under its protection with control of foreign relations. Today, along with Sabah, formerly British North Borneo, it forms part of Malaysia.

Imperialism 1815–80 and Marx

British imperial expansion, in India especially, was not interrupted by the Napoleonic wars; and as country after country fell into Napoleon's hands, their overseas possessions — Java among them — became legitimate prey for Britannia. When the wars were nearing their end, and peace terms came up for discussion, the Tory cabinet displayed a virtuous willingness to give back acquisitions taken from previous owners. A memorandum of 26 December 1813 disclaimed any wish to keep these 'for their mere commercial value', and professed a desire instead to 'give other States an additional motive to cultivate the arts of peace.'[18] In plainer terms, conservative Europe had been terrified, first by the French Revolution and then by the Bonapartist domination, and it was now vital for governments to close their ranks against any further such calamities. (A new European war almost broke out within a few months.) Colonies might be thought of not as the apples of discord they had been in the past, but as encouragements to orderly co-existence.

Between 1815 and 1880, when the 'Age of Imperialism' is conventionally supposed to have begun, industry was spreading in Europe and the USA and stimulating commercial activities and the hunt for markets and raw materials. In some areas outside Europe these could be found without forcible occupation; but this was only possible where people had already been familiarised with modern ways, having been so to speak predigested by earlier foreign rule. Britain's economic ascendency in Argentina, and for that matter in Portugal, was among the very few examples of how financial strength could confer an 'informal' authority. Even in such cases there had to be armed force in reserve in case of need. Nowhere in Asia, and still less in Africa, was such a relationship possible. Britain's conquest of India was completed by the seizure of the Punjab in 1849. France was soon busy in north Africa, which it considered its own backyard; the opening shot was the storming of that old piratical nest, Algiers, in 1830.

With steam to fill the sails and open up more of the world, there could seem to be room for all, and disputes were kept within bounds. Britain was far the biggest gainer, but once free trade became its watchword it could declare that it was not trying to keep competitors out of its preserves, but only to prevent them from keeping British enterprise out. Of course ownership brought other perquisites, such as land for settlers and local troops for hiring; in soldiers India was inexhaustible. Indeed India may be said to have made it practicable for Britain to adopt and adhere to free trade.

There were benefits for commoners as well as for their superiors; the best were the new homes offered by overseas countries like New Zealand. There were very many who disliked their stepmotherly homeland enough to make very long voyages to get away from it, the biggest number to the USA. Their betters were happy to see them go, and their exodus goes far to explaining why Britain in the second half of the nineteenth century was so little troubled by class strife. 'Our colonies are splendid fields,' said a writer on Spain in 1851, three years before another upheaval there, 'for the active spirits who create revolutions in other countries' to find new homes in.[19] So apparent was this that J.S. Mill was surprised in 1870 by 'the indifference of official people in England about retaining the colonies.'[20]

Ministers were still often noblemen, civil servants were always gentlemen; emigrants might be disgruntled radicals, although, a redeeming touch, they were quickly converted to sounder views when there were natives to be forced off the land to make room for them. They left relatives at home, sometimes small farmers forced off *their* land, who might look forward to following them. The rank and file of the army were jobless workers likewise with relatives to wish them success in battle. In 1857 the Indian Mutiny set the seal on an alliance of classes coming in sight since the failure of Chartism. In Edinburgh dramatic performances by soldiers of episodes like the storming of Lucknow drew applauding crowds.[21] An outburst of Russian chauvinism was set off by the Polish rebellion of 1863.

Marx and Engels lived through a good part of this epoch, most of the time in England, and might have been expected to take a more specific interest in empire-building and to try to fit it into the anatomy of capitalism which they were exploring, and their panorama of world history. Their standpoint however must be called Eurocentric. They saw their Europe as the continent where the most decisive developments were taking place at present, like those of 1848–9 in which they were passionately engaged. About how history was shaping outside, Marx with some aid from Engels wrote extensively, but chiefly in the form of articles designed to earn a few dollars from the American press; often extremely interesting, but seldom concerned with fundamentals of theory.

In all issues relating to Europe and the world, his concern was with political facts far more than economic theories. He may be said on the whole to have taken for granted that both Englishmen and Russians, like Romans before them, had an innate fondness for grabbing whatever they could from weaker peoples, or compelling these to labour for them — just as richer classes did with poorer classes at home. Satisfied with this commonsense approach, he would be likely to consider Russian expansion in inner Asia as something too elementary to call for elaborate analysis. As to its effects, he was wholeheartedly approving. It would relieve Europe from some of the reactionary pressures that the Tsarist police state put on it; and to Turkestan it would bring some gleams, however feeble, of modern civilisation.

India was more problematical. It was a good distance removed from barbarism, yet it appeared to have come to a halt, paralysed by chronic conflict scarcely rising above the feudal or sectarian. Nothing less than Western intrusion, dearly paid for as it might be, could jolt this ancient country out of its rut. But Marx was a man of ardent feeling, and when gazing from afar at the Mutiny he could not be entirely dispassionate. Sepoys were peasants rebelling against foreign despotism. He found it hard not to be on their side. Yet they had few intelligent leaders or ideas of progress, even by comparison with the German peasant rebels of 1525 whom Engels had written about in 1850.

About China less was known, but Marx thought about it in much the same way as about India. Peasant revolts had multiplied, but radical change could begin only with the first Opium War in 1839–42. An old worm-eaten China could survive while it remained in isolation; now that England had brought this to a violent end, dissolution of the old order must follow and make way for a Chinese revolution.[22] This was indeed to come about, if only after a whole century of painful ordeals. It was enough for Marx that history was being set free, like an unchained river that must sooner or later find its right course. Optimism about the future, little as it may seem justified by his view of the human past, was a basic part of his philosophy. It is worth noting that in late 1859 he believed the impending new war with China to be 'anything but popular with the British commercial classes;'[23] though it was the consequences of the attack for China, rather than its causes, that interested him.

1880–1914: The Age of Imperialism?

Marx died in 1883, early in the period that was to be looked back on as the apogee of imperialism; Engels lived until 1895, chiefly occupied with other matters. It may be asked whether Marx, had he lived longer, would have recognised that he had entered a qualitatively distinct epoch of modern history; or whether it was simply the time when Europeans grew more conscious of themselves as masters of the world, and were asking themselves what the outcome of their ambitions was going to be. Certainly there was an increasing volume of publicity for colonial questions, louder patriotic noise from press and pulpit and parade ground. Herbert Spencer took note in 1876 of a reviving militarism, and again in 1882: 'our illustrated papers are, week after week, occupied with little else than scenes of warfare.'[24] In 1859 a volunteer movement had been set up to meet panic fear of a French invasion; Engels was an oddly enthusiastic member. Excitement went on swelling after 1871, when Napoleon III became a harmless refugee in England. Colonial rivalries fed it, and in due time Germany replaced France as the arch-enemy.

Each stage of colonialism helped to open the way to the next. Control of India, and of points along the coast of China, made available an immense fresh store of labour to take the place of African slavery, in the shape of Indian and Chinese 'coolies,' or indentured labourers, ready for work at minimal cost everywhere from Peruvian sugar plantations to Malayan tin mines. New industries and technologies might stand in need of colonial materials like rubber or oil. Population growth was a stimulant. Every strand in the complex was interwoven with all the others. It was a further element in Europe's chaotic advance that its nations, closely related in a single culture, were yet at very diverse stages of development. East and West were ill-balanced; Germany and Italy, in the middle, were late comers, eager to catch up, and the former doing so at a perilous speed. Armies were moving towards universal instead of selective conscription, not least because of their usefulness as a school where plebeians could be licked into shape, taught docility.[25] Immense stocks of arms of all sorts were required, and supplied a welcome reinforcement to business profits.

Africa was the only continent with large areas still open in 1880, and being unexplored investment in these was risky. At the Berlin Conference in 1885 it proved possible to agree on a rough and ready partition. In China something like a gentlemen's agreement over 'spheres of influence' came about, Britain as usual contenting itself with the lion's share, the Yangtze valley. Eventually Japan was to come closest to supremacy in the Far East, thanks not to the businessman's capital, of which it had little, but to the samurai's sword; victory over China in 1894, Russia in 1904–5, invasion of China in the 1930s. Japan itself was for years a sufferer from Western dictation, apart from the initial bombardments; the 'unequal treaties' it had been compelled to sign forbade it for years to raise its tariffs in order to foster infant industries. Pettifogging Western traders were more responsible for this than any big manufacturers.

If all the capitalists greedy for colonies had been obliged to pay the costs out of their own pockets, a cooler estimate of their value might have prevailed. To a great extent it was not the profiteers who had to pay, but the ordinary public so fond of waving its national flag. John Brewer has shown how this was managed for very long in Britain through indirect taxation, with beer and tobacco as the favourite targets.[26] The real puzzle of imperialism is why the workman, now armed with a vote, was so willing to go on contributing to the empire, with every glassful he drank or pipeful he smoked. It was one of the grievances of the national movement now on the march in India that taxpayers there too had to pay, since empire-building campaigns, even far away, were officially considered to be part of the defence of India. It was intended that the expense of occupying the Sudan should be charged to Egypt. This time the bill was too heavy, Egypt too poor, and Britain had to pay a good deal.[27] France made use of native conscripts, in their homelands or in other people's.

Psychologically as well as in other ways colonial mastery could help to inflate the self-esteem of ruling classes and reassure them of their natural right to go on ruling at home. In nineteenth-century Britain it must have been a weighty factor in giving the old landed oligarchy the will and ability to go on directing political as well as social life, instead of letting itself be put on the shelf. For Europe's disinherited masses who were being deprived of the extensive lands formerly owned in common, by processes like the Enclosures in England, there may have been a kind of consolation in being able to think of Burmese or Tasmanian dreamlands as 'ours', a restoration of the lost national patrimony. Lord Acton remarked on the 'intense desire', 'diseased and guilty longing' of all Frenchmen for any and every territory that could by hook or by crook be annexed.[28] Their kings had created France by toilsome adding of province to province, while peasants spent their lives struggling to add an acre or two to their cramped farms.

P.K. O'Brien ends a balance-sheet of costs and profits by saying that Britain's 'gentlemanly capitalists' reaped most of the gains of empire, while the masses 'cheerfully and even proudly shouldered a tax bill for an empire from which they derived very little', in hard cash at least, for decades before and after 1914.[29] When costs began to mount, and went on mounting, the very rich might be taken aback by the prospect of having to pay a trifle more themselves, out of their vast unearned incomes. In 1902 the Tory Chancellor, Sir Michael Hicks Beach, an economist of the old school, resigned and wrote an alarming memorandum on the strain that the national finances were coming under. His leader Lord Salisbury shared his anxiety, but could only comment: 'When I saw how blindly the heads of our defensive departments surrendered themselves to the fatal guidance of their professional advisers, I realised that we were in face of a Jingo hurricane, and were driving before it under bare poles.'[30]

There could scarcely be a plainer confession of political bankruptcy; Salisbury's 'bare poles' were a faithful image of Tory statesmanship. Such prophets of doom could regard themselves as vindicated when seven years later an impudent young Welsh chancellor wanted them to contribute to social services, of all things, and told the country that it cost as much to keep one duke in comfort for a year as a pair of warships. Toryism like Bismarck had in part been pushed into 'Jingo' policies by the clamour of the business classes — now joining it under the title of 'Unionists' — who stood to profit by empire expenses, the heavier the better; and of course by the professional advisers or military experts. There was besides a reversal of former suspicions of private enterprise. Over Sarawak there had at least been long and anxious thought about the propriety of adding private acquisitions to the empire. Now buccaneers like Rhodes were being turned loose on Africa, while Sabah was handed over for exploitation to a 'British North Borneo Company', or privatised.

To sustain the prestige of monarchy as a bulwark against socialism was an objective wherever thrones were still standing. Empire-drummers rescued Queen Victoria from the unpopularity she had fallen into since the death of Prince Albert. Fear of socialism was sharpest in Germany where the working class was the best organised and the fastest growing. For most Germans the Hohenzollerns were newcomers, strangers, who had to bang their own drum to make themselves heard. Logically the best place for a flow of German capital abroad would have been an industrialising Russia, but to Bismarck this mattered less than fear of Russia's enemy, the Hapsburg empire, crumbling if not propped up by Germany, and leaving Germany hemmed in by a Slav ocean. Monarchy was learning to save up for a rainy day, and Nicholas II's hope of private profit from timber on the Korean border may have done much to get Russia into war with Japan.

Each of the Great Powers was being seized by the fear of isolation, and a web of secret treaties was being spread over the continent. Germany and Austria-Hungary joined hands in 1879, France and Russia, more astonishingly, in 1891, Britain joined them in 1907. There had been an Anglo-French crisis in 1892–3 over Siam (Thailand), another over the Eastern Sudan in 1897, and an Anglo-Russian crisis ending in 1895 over some strategic mountains in the Himalayas. By the time of the Franco-German crises over Morocco in 1906 and 1911 Europe had entered the stage when an explosion would involve everyone. Compared with its cost when it came in 1914 the market value of all the empires was trifling. The real causes lay in the tensions fastening on a sick Europe, and those at work within each individual country.

Among the human agents who were to translate these tensions into action, the fighting men were naturally in the foreground. In some armies, especially the British, colonial campaigns might be called their bread and butter. A young English officer starting on his duties in India between the wars felt that his pay must have been calculated with mathematical precision as the minimum needed to keep him alive and fit for work.[31] To many generations of aspirants like him only war could bring medals and promotion. Russian frontier officers, or Britons on the North-west Frontier in earlier days, were often suspected of helping to get a campaign going. At the top of the ladder we see the general in Conan Doyle's story 'The Green Flag' preparing happily for the battle he is about to fight in Africa, and to the peerage and the £100,000 honorarium it will bring him. On the civil side there was the same desire to see frontiers pushed out as wide as possible. An Indian historian points out that officials often had a financial stake in what was going on, even when firm evidence of their being influenced by these may be lacking.[32]

When Upper Burma was annexed in 1886 there were rumours of the then Viceroy of India having an interest in timber. It may have been near the end, when colonies were restlessly awaiting independence, that the 'Services', the men on the spot, did most harm, by obstructing change. In this the French army was the most criminal of all.

At the bottom of the heap we can count the workers who made the weapons, built and repaired the warships and planes. Krupp workmen were said to feel a feudal or filial attachment to their employer, and William II himself visited them and gingered them up with fiery speeches. Naval ports were notoriously bellicose. British arms dealers depended a good deal for their market on colonial garrisons and campaigns. Workers in the USA were talked into support of the Vietnam war and its ferocious bombing of civilians with the argument that peace would mean a slump in the arms industry and an end to the golden days of 'the full dinner-pail'.

The new popular press was another ally, working singlemindedly for its own profits, but finding empire excitements, like those of sex, a rewarding field. Religion and empire were as always arm in arm. By 1900 missionary activity was nearing its watershed, in Europe the religion of the churches was already on its long downward slide. Empire might might seem the best means of slowing this. Clamorous noises from the far outposts could often be counted on to muffle the fainter voice of reason. Robinson and Gallagher usefully stress the part played by the converging effects of Irish Home Rule, Egypt, and Britain's defeat by the Boers at Majuba, in splitting the Liberal party.[33]

A reader may still find Norman Angell's *The Great Illusion*, of 1910, enough to alarm him with doubts about human sanity. Much of it is an anthology of harebrained folly and ignorance among the braying, bellowing chorus of imperialists all over Europe. Their rockbottom conviction was the antique Colbertian one that the world had room only for a fixed volume of trade, so that whatever share one nation gets of it, another loses. Each must be ready to fight for whatever colonies it can grab. Angell had no objection to empires in principle: one could only do business where law and order were respected, and where they were not, some civilised state should step in to guarantee them. Which government was to undertake the effort was of no consequence. He gave up his editorial career to expound his doctrine, and was later a Labour MP.

The philosophic Schopenhauer had contemplated with pity the spectacle of China, 'threatened by rebellion within and foes without', the penalty for having cultivated only peaceful ways and 'ignored the arts of war'.[34] He failed to see that the cure for rebellion would have been reform, not the headman's axe so plentifully employed. Among lesser minds, propagandists like General von Bernhardi, a belief seems to have been spreading that an empire must not only know how to repel attack, but must go on expanding indefinitely, or else lose vitality and wilt. To fulfil such needs idealism had to be contorted into some curious shapes. 'We live in an age,' two of Rhodes's ruffians sighed, 'when sentiment is out of fashion and cynicism the vogue.' They were extolling their master's invasion of Matabeleland in 1893, which ran into strong resistance, and lamenting that soulless Little Englanders would dismiss the fallen as mere adventurers.[35] There was certainly cynicism enough among the managers of such enterprises; between it and gullible sentimentality the gap can seldom in history have been wider.

Left-wing critics

The bombardment of Alexandria and occupation of Egypt by a Liberal ministry headed by 'that great and good man' Mr Gladstone, in 1882, might seem to mark a new departure. So it did, in the increasing subordination of government to stock exchange in Britain; in economic terms, since what was at stake in Egypt was money lent by financiers to a bankrupt potentate, it was a regression from productive industry to parasitic usury. Capitalism is a very fluid system, able to adapt itself itself to official directives when obliged to, or to regional habits and mobile social relations; all these count for more than any inner intrinsic evolutionary impulse, or *élan vital*, except of course the primordial appetite for money. In England the lead was moving from the north and manufacture to the south or Home Counties and finance, with a seasoning of fox-hunting, country-house life and the long English weekend.

Aristocracy, or gentility, had been saved from any radical follow-up to the Reform of 1832 by the industrialists' fear of the new working class they were bringing into the world. They might well be nervous, alone as they were at first in Europe. They could only put their trust in the protection of the old landed ruling class, familiar with the management of an army, and able to mobilise a rustic yeomanry as counterweight to any urban crowd. Now political entente was leading to a new social formation, a plutocracy, a fusion likely to bring out the less desirable qualities on each side. Royal families here and elsewhere provided a coping-stone. Even in hard-working Germany it was easier for Jewish than for Christian businessmen to get themselves ennobled, because most of them were financiers, which gave them closer contact with Court circles.[36]

Worsening international relations by the end of the century had portents in the conflict between Spain and America in 1898, and the Boer War of 1899–1902; these were wars between white peoples, even if fought far away. J.A. Hobson's very influential book *Imperialism*, in 1902, was concerned very much with the protracted struggle for the gold mines of South Africa. Though a liberal, not a socialist, he was arguing that the underlying cause had been an unwholesome excess of capital exports to such regions. This was due to the fact that wealth at home was maldistributed, so that the masses had too little purchasing power for the capitalists to be tempted to employ their money in building factories to produce goods for them to buy.

This has been criticised as an explanation of imperialism on the ground that most of the outflow of capital from Britain was not going to 'colonial' or Afro-Asian areas, but into others already in process of development, two-thirds of it between 1900 and 1913 to North or South America.[37] O'Brien holds that competition, German and American foremost, was forcing Britain to think more of its colonies: 'exports of capital became slowly but perceptibly more concentrated upon the empire' (but again, largely to the dominions). Still, taking the whole period 1846–1914, he doubts whether the empire 'made any positive long-term contribution to the health of the domestic economy,' though no doubt it enriched individuals. For the majority of people Hobson seems to have been right in thinking that 'the empire represented an increasingly costly alternative to social reform.'[38]

It might be costly for some colonies too. India was growing poorer, nationalists maintained, and their 'Drain theory' of a chronic yearly appropriation of resources by the British implied that really capital was being transferred not from Britain to India, but from India to Britain, whence some of it might be sent off again to America and be invested more profitably there.

How Hobson's sweeping social change was to be brought about he had no clear idea. When Lenin, a gloomy exile in wartime Zurich, took up the subject, the missing link was ready to hand in the form of social revolution. He made enthusiastic use of Hobson's thesis, and built his own *Imperialism* of 1916 very much on its foundations. This gave him a means of denouncing the war and all the combatants. He had found a strictly economic interpretation of modern war such as Marx had never looked for. This narrowing was not Lenin's own choice; he was writing for the Russian public, accustomed by long practice to read between the lines, and censorship would debar him from publishing anything about the war in political language. He could not always sound quite impartial but had to stack his cards somewhat. His Hobsonian approach had other drawbacks. Since 1902 the concentration of capital into fewer and fewer hands had been much less rapid in Britain or France, the arch-colonialists, than in Germany or America. Tsarist Russia could not be accused of exporting capital; it imported a great deal instead. Britain and France were the two great moneylenders, and had got Turkey so heavily in debt that the Turks joined Germany against them in October 1914 to shake off the chain, as well as in the hope of recovering Egypt.

Whatever the deficiencies of Lenin's treatise, it became the standard Marxist doctrine on imperialism, and a test of orthodoxy, because soon after writing it Lenin led the first successful socialist revolution. Professor Postan, who disapproved of that revolution, once told me that although he thought the book's argument wrong, he considered it a model of methodology. As an opponent of Marxism he liked to see historical theory rendered harmless by being deprived of its political half and reduced to economic determinism. Another dictum of his was that 'What Bismarck said is not history' — it is the price of potatoes that matters.

In the years before 1914 German socialists were the ones most interested in questions of war and imperialism. Their government, as well as

Austria's, was still monarchical and did not even pretend, like Britain's, that its foreign policies were decided by public opinion. Socialists therefore were apt to blame autocracy for their country's oppressive militarism and, after Bismarck, its adventures in imperialism; though there were some in the party, among them the revisionist Bernstein, who thought that their country ought to have an empire like the rest. In the realm of theory the leading figure was Karl Kautsky, who had been tutored by Engels. He went on rejecting colonialism altogether and was horrified by the prospect of a European war. He was impressed by Hobson, but not to the point of ascribing all evils of imperialism to capitalism, or identifying the two dragons as some other socialists were ready to do. Political or sociological thinking was his favourite field — as we should have to say of Marx too had he not entangled himself for so long in his labyrinthine study of capitalism. In Kautsky's view imperialism was a necessity for some capitalists rather than for capitalism as a whole. It was in general a political more than an economic consequence of capitalism, as, for instance, in the 1907 election when the conservative parties won votes from the Social Democrats by rattling sabres and accusing them of want of patriotism.[39]

Kautsky was again impressed in 1910, but with similar reservations, by Rudolf Hilferding, who may be called the most acute analyst of the German species of imperialism. It was that of a new country in a hurry and therefore moving towards forms of combinations or amalgamation, the 'monopoly capitalism' which Marx had predicted. This was accompanied, as it has been in all coutries bent on speedy industrialisation except America, by close links between industry and state. In Germany this worked largely through what Hilferding called 'finance capitalism', by which he meant an interlocking of industrial with banking capital under official guidance. Capital was scarce, and had to be made to work for the nation, instead of being frittered away in Stock Exchange speculation. Military habits, the ideal of an entire people advancing at the word of command, made this a congenial development. Strength, leading towards prosperity, counted more than freedom. Baulked of political primacy, the bourgeoisie was the more intent on pushing its way forward by dint of moneybags. In return Bismarck was the first head of government to make his aristocratic diplomats serve as travelling salesmen for German exports.

By 1914, it has been said, Hobson, Angell and Brailsford had put together something not far short of 'A coherent body of doctrine about finance, imperialism and foreign policy.'[40] This is putting rather too much weight on the British contribution; imperialism along with capitalism would flow into different channels. Often what has been meant by it is simply a mood of aggressively competitive search for wealth and power and a readiness to risk war for their sake. Its unthinking bluster is engendered by social divisions that need such rhetoric to disguise them. If this is what we mean, no analysis half as subtle and intricate as Rosa Luxemburg's of 1913 is needed. 'The psychology of imperialism,' Leonard Woolf wrote, 'is only an extension or development of the psychology of nationalism'.[41] This implies that it is fundamentally irrational and therefore constitutes one of modern life's basic problems, or obstacles to human survival.

National Socialism

Bismarck may have been pushed into half-hearted colonialism chiefly as a carrot for middle-class opposition. His own feeling, he proclaimed, was that Germany was now 'sated', and needed nothing more. But William II, who got rid of him in 1890, and many others were not; in his reign the spectre of Nazism can already be seen lurking. Kaiser Bill and Corporal Adolf were both thunderous demagogues, melodramatic speechifiers; Nazism would carry Wilhelmine Germany to its logical or crazy extreme. Dead men like Nietzsche provided the war cries, the Third Reich obeyed them.

In the slump years it was the lower middle classes, it appears, that provided a mass following for Nazism, as it had done in Britain for jingoism. Such a social formation or random multitude could have no ideology or leadership of its own. Its situation was deteriorating, and fanned an impulse towards anarchic violence. Nazism might in fact be called a petty bourgeoisie running amuck. It is the most erratic or malleable class because of its lack of any identity of its own, and hence is the more ready, along with elements of the better-off middle classes, to evade bewildering difficulties by leaving thinking and responsibility to one inspired man, as recommended by Thomas Carlyle. For cognate reasons, the same class has been the most fertile in gifted, original individuals.

No one could have any clear notion of which way the Nazi party was going. It was a saying among adherents (probably of the better-off sort, like the one I heard it from) that the longer you were in the party the more moderate you became, and the most moderate man in it was Adolf Hitler. Upper-class Germany could afford to assume that no serious harm would come to it from such a movement. Police, army, law courts made no real effort to check Nazi violence against opponents on the left. Capitalism did not launch Nazism, nor back it strongly until the more respectable national-conservative parties had tried and failed to cope with the slump and there was no choice left. When Nazism came to power and set up its concentration camps, well-dressed Germans can scarcely be blamed for an indulgent attitude so widely shared by the well-to-do of Western Europe, among them the Emperor of India.

Hitler's great achievement was that he found the German people deeply disillusioned with war and everything connected with it, and in a few years re-educated it into the most militarist nation, along with the Japanese, on earth. He had six or seven years in power to extinguish all opposition or criticism before it was time to go to war. Education meant indoctrination, and seven annual classes of school-leavers had been subjected to it by 1939, as six more were before the war ended. 'Already in school I was a soldier', one young prisoner said proudly. The youngest were the most blindly devoted to the cause, the 'War for Freedom' as a patriotic song called it. Some juvenile divisions were formed and sent to the Eastern Front when it was coming under strain. Hitler was delighted with their performance: 'They fight fantastically well!' It might be thought that some German instinct of self-destruction, self-sacrifice to some monstrous deity, was at work. British troops were astonished to learn that the Germans they encountered in North Africa were not an élite corps, but ordinary run-of-the-mill recruits. It seems they felt no need of religion, of which Dr Goebbels was an implacable enemy. Stalin took pains to have God on his side; with the Fuehrer in command no God was required.

The Nazi era is entitled to be looked back on as a distinct phase in the evolution of imperialism. It was the greatest effort at European domination since Napoleon, and it was far more than a simple effort by a successful commander to exploit a post-revolutionary situation. In its perverted way National Socialism really was socialistic, because its aim was prosperity for the entire *Volk*, the primitive tribe with all divisions exorcised. Officers and rank-and-file ate the same rations. Had the war been won the victorious armies would have been able to demand their reward, as those of the late Roman Republic did. Churchill was upheld by a conviction of the sacredness of the British Empire, but he felt no discrepancy between this and the large number of Britons mouldering in East End slums. For Nazism, the whole *Volk* was to be lifted up above common humanity, at the expense of other races created for its service or to be cleared out of its way. Compared with this all-consuming drive to power, British jingoism was a mere frolic or carnival. But the white settler attitude to coloured populations had a strong likeness to Nazism. There is a lesson here that socialism must always be firmly internationalist, or it may turn into something horribly different.

Heine's prophecy that some day the peaceful German would wake up like a sleeping giant and seize his hammer had come true. When the hammer broke, it was discovered that there had been no Nazis in any district investigated, though some had been heard of elsewhere. Germans seemed very much like what they had always been, and before long, with American nursing, were more prosperous than ever. Capitalism was firmly in the saddle again, the Churches were placidly installed in their wonted place. Such dizzy alternations make history harder to chart.

Capitalist Utopia

Europe, having proved incapable of building anything better than a world fit for heroes to be killed in, left it to the half-European outsider, the USA, to take the lead in inaugurating a half-new one. America had a different formation from both of the two main earlier capitalist types, Anglo-French and German-Japanese. It was free of aristocracy or any traditional bent towards colonialism, except within its own promised land of North America. It had no powerful rivals nearby and had got along in peacetime without a big army. At the end of the nineteenth century it sounded a new note, with a call for an open door into China for all with wares to sell: Chinese approval was taken for granted. Its commercial strength enabled it to do without colonies, so long as it was not shut out from those of its competitors. After 1945 it wanted them to give up their colonies and merge their interests with its own. The parallel political aim was that of gathering them all into a permanent alliance against Communism.

Kautsky had theorised about a coming time of 'ultra-imperialism,' a time beyond any separate empires, and since the Second World War some such transition could seem to be taking place, with the 'multinational corporation' as its propeller. Some participants, like fascist Spain and Portugal, were of the most unsavoury type, but their anti socialism was beyond question. Through such murky channels the poisoned breath of pre-war days could still find a way in, just as much of the atmosphere of before 1914 lingered after the First World War. The Third World too was being brought into line, to prevent subversive influences from finding a foothold. As in the Roman empire, all local élites and governing groups were to be enrolled as collaborators. This may have helped to give rise to a hypothesis mooted of late, which puts the blame for all modern imperialism on to wily collaborators, beguiling the innocent foreigner into serving their purposes. It is of course true that imperialism has always needed local agents, but only in second place. They profited by the empires, they now profit by the American hegemony; they are not the originators.

Indirect means of control have been preferred, and dictators, usually self-promoted army men, have played a sterling part. The hegemony has not always made its choice in a logical manner, because it inherits from history too many contradictions or eccentricities, and has been led astray by its Cold War fixation. Pakistan, ruled most of the time by safe military men, has been preferred to democratic India, which until lately has declined, like Japan, to give free entry to American goods; Pakistan has had to rely on US loans and arms. In Afghanistan America has aided Pakistan to back the fighting forces of Islamic fanaticism, long after the Soviet withdrawal. Yet to any complaints against Israel it can only repeat, in the words of Isaiah: 'Speak ye comfortably to Jerusalem; say unto her, that her iniquities are pardoned.'

A mean-looking shop in a New York street carries, or it used to, the grandiloquent title 'Paramount Pawnbrokers Inc.', as if echoing Britain's old claim to 'paramountcy' in India. Today it is more likely to remind the passer-by that the USA has become the grand pawnbroker or moneylender of the globe. Nowadays financial power means also the military power which Washington has made such potent use of. An incongruous but winning image of Uncle Sam as Plato's philosopher-king, or Confucius's benign mandarin, has for many years been provided by the spaceship *Enterprise* and its crew, with assimilated aliens among them, to say nothing of a robot. They have nothing to do with commercial enterprise or raw materials; to extend human knowledge is their mission. They are careful never to tamper with the customs or beliefs of any race, but they come across some very freakish or bellicose ones, and try patiently to smooth out their feuds.

Still, the *Enterprise* has a sting of its own to defend itself with if molested. Even in a model school punishments have to be handed out at times, and presidents have to show that they are not to be trifled with. A Kipling story of the post-1918 era, 'As Easy as ABC', predicted a world board of control keeping order everywhere with the aid of the newly invented bombing plane. When the USA set out to provide this service it took little thought for the enormous amount of damage that might have to be inflicted, as in Korea and Vietnam, without the purposed aim being fulfilled. Notwithstanding this, Kissinger and his circle, with their own professional axe to grind, could argue that the bombing of Hanoi was vital to the security of America.[42] Libya was bombarded, Grenada and Panama occupied. When Salman Rushdie visited Nicaragua he heard that the CIA's 1986–7 budget for putting the screw on a nation of under three million inhabitants was eight hundred million dollars.[43] In the Gulf War a great many of a tyrant's subjects were killed and maimed, but the tyrant was left to continue unscathed. Elimination of even the worst dictator may bring awkward problems of replacement.

'Terrorism' has come by incessant repetition to signify illegal resistance to authority, usually that of the hegemony; but its historic meaning is government by violence and intimidation. This is what the rule of the hegemony, or its understrappers, has too often been. D.H. Lawrence maintained that under the bland surface consciousness of America there was a destructive inner layer. 'The American has got to destroy. It is his destiny.'[44] If so, it may be traceable to the wholesale destruction of forests and their inhabitants that accompanied the march from Atlantic to Pacific, the first hegemony.

At any rate, in the midst of much brave official talk about human rights, the practice of torture has been spreading across a great part of the world, often with the connivance, at least, of Washington. Its fresh growth has had roots, Hobsbawm points out, in colonial conflict.[45] While upholding the cause of the Algerians fighting against the French, Fanon had to regret their frequent resort to primitive brutality, usually against their fellow-countrymen, easier targets than the French.[46] Torture was being used more systematically by the French, as it had been by the Nazis against the French Resistance, and habits were bred that have flared up again in today's erratic massacres in Algeria. Responsible ministers in many lands have shown a ghoulish readiness to shut their eyes, if no more, to savageries not long ago deemed unthinkable. In September 1996 the Pentagon made public, a trifle shamefacedly, training manuals used in the US academy for Latin American army and police officers, in which beatings, torture and secret executions were recommended.[47] On 5 October 1997 television's Channel 4 showed a grim set of interviews with men who had participated in tortures, and pictures of some of the things that happened.

Swollen arms industries are an integral part of the hegemony, whose output has to find many of its markets abroad, many of them headed by autocrats or dictators. Meanwhile production of goods for use has been increasingly left to some Third World countries within the American-Japanese orbit, as beneath the white man's dignity. In September 1982 Britain's Tory premier was in Japan pleading with business leaders to invest more in Britain. Capital exports can be either enslaving or stimulating; it depends on what sort of country they are going to. British investments and loans helped the US to grow. For British financiers, free to put their capital wherever they like, buying up real estate in Los Angeles may be more congenial than managing troublesome factories at home.

It has been suggested that Hobson's forecast of an idle rentier West living on a hard-working East, fuelled by Western capital and technology, was not so much wrong as premature. In the earlier stages, in South Korea for example, success depended on a military man with an American army to lean on. It may be that the watchful American eye helped to keep industry and profits expanding; and as in Japan, America enforced a helpful agrarian reform, as the Britain of the landlords never did. It seems also that growth can have a certain self-righting tendency in such conditions, extending prosperity, and by slower degrees civic freedom, to lower classes as well. We may be drifting, in short, into novel latitudes.

Of the East Asian 'tigers' and their imitators, Japan and Korea were true nations with long histories, though Korea lost its independence a century ago. The others are artificial communities, called into existence by imperialism at one stage or another. Singapore and Hong Kong were bare rocks until Britain took hold of them, the latter chiefly as a smuggling base for opium and other goods, and attracted flocks of migrant Chinese to them. Taiwan too was peopled mainly by immigrants from China; it and Korea both belonged to the Japanese empire. Malaya was assembled by Britain from Malay, Indian and Chinese materials; Indonesia is a vast Dutch collection of miscellaneous islands and races. These beginnings have left them readier for new initiatives than old nations sunk in fixed habits like Britain. The US grew up with similar elasticities.

These new countries have been easily Americanised (though not much more easily than western Europe) and initiated into the 'American way of life', with its blue jeans, hamburgers, jazz bands, television and gadgetry of all kinds. This has all helped to bind the new Utopia together, in a manner not apparently achieved by socialist China or the new capitalist China with its strategic outpost Tibet, or that storehouse of minerals, Sinkiang. Everywhere else men and women have American dreams, and believe that they may come true, even if they may not always relish Washington's way of doing things. We may call this 'cultural imperialism,' if we wish, but no force has been needed to impose it. A surrealistic reflection can be seen in our knowledge that whatever number of light years the *Enterprise* may travel, it will find good American spoken on every planet, and will never have the bother of learning any other language. Still, scientists or fantasists are talking now of trillions of inhabitable planets, a great many with intelligent life. On our own planet it often seems that intelligent life has yet to appear, except in negligible numbers.

Lately the collapse of the USSR has thrown open a vast field to a new species of imperialism, freedom for Western predators and their Eastern sharers to make fortunes out of the wreckage of socialist achievements.[48] Against this we can set a series of restitutions to some of the worst-off of humanity, the aboriginal populations pushed down by modern imperialism after some had already been banished into the wildernesses by earlier conquerors, as in India and the Americas, and are only now re-emerging into the light of day. A number of small hill peoples on India's north-east frontier have won autonomy, after sporadic guerrilla fighting. The Guaraní speakers of Paraguay have had their language recognised as a second national one, alongside Spanish. Characteristically perhaps, the USA has authorised Amerindians to open gambling saloons on tribal territory, where white men can flock to throw away their money. Aborigines in Australia and Maoris in New Zealand have been given back some of their old lands. Most striking of all, Canada is erecting an immense area of its northlands into a national home for the Inuits, to be called Nunavut, 'Our Land'.[49]

As for the long sought 'interpretation,' imperialism has proved too many-sided and chaotic a subject for any categorical solution, even for a single chosen period. We must take leave of what used to be dogmatically called 'the Marxist theory', with the same respectful firmness as the Hegelian triad.

Notes

1. I am indebted to a paper prepared in March 1955 at the Royal Institute of International Affairs, 'Sarawak. The Political and Economic Background'.
2. The documents cited in the Record Office belong to the Foreign Office volume FO 12.35, 'Sir James Brooke's proposals respecting Sarawak', 1852–69.
3. Memorandum by Mellish, 28 November 1852.
4. Dona Torr, *Karl Marx on China 1852–1860*, London, 1951, p.49n.
5. St John, 11 January 1958.
6. Cochrane, on the *Niger*, 16 June 1858, forwarded from Colonial Office.
7. Report forwarded by Admiralty, 6 September 1858.
8. Letter from Brooke, 19 March 1858, and minute, 9 April 1858.
9. Admiralty 15 December 1858, with report from Commander Cresswell.
10. With a hydrography report, 27 January 1859.
11. Ibid., 12 December 1859.
12. Memorandum by A.H. Layard, 2 January 1862.
13. Government of India, 16 August 1862, enclosing correspondence with the Governor of Singapore.
14. 8 January 1863.
15. Minute by Clarendon, 9 February 1866.
16. Ibid., 21 January 1867.
17. Ibid., 10 June 1869.
18. C.K. Webster (ed.), *British Diplomacy 1813–1815. Select Documents*, London, 1921, p.127.
19. G.A. Hoskins, *Spain As It Was*, London, 1851, Vol.1, p.312.
20. J.S. Mill, Letter to Judge Chapman in New Zealand, 14 January 1870.

21. James Grant, *Old and New Edinburgh*, London nd., Vol.3, p.88.
22. Dona Torr, op.cit., p.4.
23. Ibid., p.86, 18 October 1859.
24. Cited by C.K. Ogden and M.S. Florence, in *Militarism versus Feminism*, M. Kamester and J. Vellacott (eds), London, 1987.
25. See my essay on 'Conscription and Society in Europe', in M.R.D. Foot (ed.), *War and Society*, London, 1973.
26. John Brewer, *The Sinews of Power: War, Money and the English State, 1688–1783*, London, 1989.
27. Philip Magnus, *Kitchener: Portrait of an Imperialist*, 1958; Harmondsworth edn, 1988, ch.6.
28. Lord Acton, *Historical Essays*, Cambridge, 1870, ch.7.
29. P.K. O'Brien, 'The Costs and Benefits of British Imperialism, 1846–1914', in *Past and Present*, No.120, 1988, p.195.
30. J.A.R. Marriot, *England since Waterloo*, London, 1913, pp.180–1.
31. Brig. Gen. John Prendergast, *Prender's Progress: A Soldier in India, 1931–47*, London, 1979, ch.1.
32. D.R. Sardesai, *British Trade Expansion in Southeast Asia, 1830–1914*, Delhi, 1977, pp.279–80.
33. R. Robinson and J. Gallagher, *Africa and the Victorians: The official mind of imperialism*, London, 1961, p.160.
34. A. Schopenhauer, *On Human Nature*, selected essays trans. T.B. Saunders, London, 1897, p.40.
35. W.A. Wills and L.T. Collingridge (eds), *The Downfall of Lobengula*, London, 1894, p.239.
36. Dominic Lieven, *The Aristocracy in Europe, 1815–1914*, New York, 1992, pp.63–4.
37. M. Barratt-Brown, *After Imperialism*, London, 1963, pp.92–5.
38. P.K. O'Brien, op.cit., pp.197–200.
39. G.P. Steenson, *Karl Kautsky 1854–1938*, Pittsburgh, 1978, pp.175, 192, 197.
40. Duncan Wilson, *Leonard Woolf, A Political Portrait*, New York, 1978, p.108.
41. Leonard Woolf, *After the Deluge. A Study of Communal Psychology*, 1931; Harmondsworth, 1938, p.258.
42. Walter Carlsnaes, *Problems of Comparative Conceptualisation*, Oxford, 1986, p.85.
43. Salman Rushdie, *The Jaguar Smile. An American Journey*, London, 1987, p.30.
44. D.H. Lawrence, *Studies in Classical American Literature*, London, 1933, pp.85–6.
45. E.J. Hobsbawm, *On History*, London, 1997, ch.20.
46. Franz Fanon, *The Wretched of the Earth*, 1961, Harmondsworth, 1967.
47. See, for example, *Guardian*, 23 September 1996.
48. See Peter Gowan, 'Crisis East and West', pamphlet No.12, in *Socialist Renewal* series, Nottingham, 1997.
49. See article by Michael Parfit in *National Geographic*, September, 1997.

I owe thanks to my wife, Heather Kiernan, for a number of valuable suggestions.

Indian Nationalism — Before and After Independence

Ralph Russell

This title doesn't really convey the range and the complexity of the issues I propose to discuss. These issues cover the fight for national liberation, both of India conceived as a single whole and of the nationalities within it, some manifestations of nationalism, and the interplay with these things of what in India is generally called communalism, i.e. consciousness of religious community. Since I am a Marxist and a communist, and since Marxists and communists form a part of my audience, I shall also discuss the relation of communist theory to these things and its not always successful attempt to come to terms with them; and at this point it is best to make clear, in very general terms, what some of the main features of this theory have been. It has always been our view, and indeed the view of most progressive people, that movements of national liberation and national self-determination should be supported, while the ideology of nationalism — of putting the aggrandisement and the supposed interests of one's nation above all other considerations — should be opposed. This remains my own very firmly held view.

Throughout the period I shall be considering, roughly the 1920s to the present day, there has been an interweaving of all the different kinds of consciousness I have spoken of but in varying degrees of prominence in different periods. I think it best to deal with things more or less chronologically. Here and there I have given my account something of an autobiographical slant and I begin with a reference of this kind.

India in the 1930s: Is India a 'nation'?

I first became aware of the importance of India in world politics after I joined the Communist Party in 1934. To those who had reached political consciousness before that its importance was quite evident. Lenin, in what we can now see was a very over-optimistic estimate, had declared that the future of socialism all over the world was assured since Russia, China and India together accounted for the majority of the world's population and all three countries were moving in that direction. R. Palme Dutt in the first edition of his book *India Today* (1940) called India 'the pivot of modern imperialism'. (p.17)

In this connection the question arose: Is India a nation? This question had an immediate practical relevance because the argument that it was not a nation was used as a weapon to discredit the movement for Indian independence. Thus Churchill in a speech made on 18 March 1931 said, 'India is a geographical term. It is no more a united nation than the Equator,' (quoted in the *Penguin Dictionary of Modern Quotations*, 1971, p.44).

I may remark in passing that Stalin's standard definition of 'nation', which I can still remember by heart, would also have excluded India. His definition runs 'a nation is a historically evolved, stable community of language, territory, economic life and psychological make-up manifested in a community of culture'. In characteristic style he continues 'It must be emphasised that none of the above characteristics is by itself sufficient to define a nation. On the other hand, it is sufficient for a single one of these characteristics to be absent and the nation ceases to be a nation.' Orthodox Stalinist though I was in those days, Stalin's insistence even then struck me as being a bit much. For example, in Ireland there are monolingual speakers of Irish and monolingual speakers of English, but on those grounds it seemed ridiculous to say the Irish were not a nation. Similarly, Lenin's praise of the official language policies pursued by Switzerland perhaps implied that despite its multi-lingual character the Swiss were a nation.

Anyway, the political needs of that period dictated that for all practical purposes India should be regarded as a nation, and both the world communist movement and the leaders of the Indian movement for independence did just that.

All problems were viewed on an all-India scale, and the major one was that of how to counter the divide-and-rule strategy of the British, expressed mainly and most effectively in the fomenting of Hindu-Muslim antagonism. Indians and British communists alike felt the need to counter this by stressing the unity of India and the united character of the movement against British rule, and this led frequently to a tendency to deny, or play down, the divisive effects of Hindu and Muslim communal consciousness. That tendency is still in evidence, and I shall return to it in a moment.

Mass mobilisation

A time came when the freedom movement realised the need to bring mass sanctions to bear against the British authorities. (I may remark in passing that the Indian National Congress, which became the main organisation of the freedom struggle, did not put mass mobilisation on its agenda until just after the First World War, about thirty years after it was founded.) When it did, different styles of achieving this came into being.

First, the communists and people like Nehru counted on appealing to the class interests of the mass of the Indian population and concentrated on bringing into existence powerful trade unions in the towns and peasant organisations in the countryside, and enlisting them in the independence struggle, arguing that only in an independent India could their legitimate demands be met. Second, an appeal to the Hindu masses could be made in Hindu terms. Thirdly, an appeal to the Muslim masses could be made in Muslim terms. And finally, an appeal (as yet in minor key) was made to the national consciousness of the different nationalities in India.

Thus several different appeals were made, and attempts were made to reconcile any divergences between them and to bring them into unison — which brings me to a consideration of the great historic role of Gandhi.

Gandhi

Gandhi was the first and only leader of the twenties and thirties to bring into being a mass all-India mobilisation behind national demands. Failure to recognise his uniqueness is a major defect in R. Palme Dutt's *India Today*. Thus, when after the end of the first great wave of struggle in 1919–22 conditions developed around 1928 for the launching of the second wave, Dutt records that 'Gandhi returned to active leadership of the Congress' and goes on to call him 'this Jonah of revolution, this general of unbroken disasters'. This estimate is not in itself seriously wrong, but it misses the point that no one who wanted a mass all-India movement could get one unless Gandhi was prepared to give it to them. There was no one else who *could* launch an all-India mass movement.

My own realisation of this came in 1943 when Gandhi announced a fast to the death against 'the leonine policies of the British government'. The Indian soldiers of whom I was at that time in command had never even heard of Nehru, but all of them knew and revered Gandhi despite the fact that Indian soldiers were, to say the least of it, not the most politically advanced section of the Indian people, since would-be recruits were screened and politically conscious ones were rejected. The general atmosphere at that time was electric, and I remember a fellow Indian officer, Sandhurst-trained and completely identified with British interests, remarking in an impeccable upper-class English accent 'If that old man dies, there will be hell to pay.' There would indeed have been hell to pay, but the fast was in fact called off.

Gandhi and the Hindu appeal

What was the basis of Gandhi's appeal? He preached Hindu-Muslim harmony, and the completeness of his sincerity in this was proved by the fact that in the end he gave his life for it when he was assassinated by a fanatical Hindu communalist. But for all that, his mass appeal was that of a simple-living Hindu holy man. He also appealed to the Hindu masses by saying that independence would restore Ram Raj. Ram, or in the usual spelling Rama, was a mythical Hindu ruler of what is now eastern Uttar Pradesh and in Hindu mythology the period of his rule was a golden age. Obviously this could make no appeal to Muslims in whose traditions the Hindu kings of the pre-Muslim era clearly did not figure. Moreover Gandhi frequently declared himself to be a devout Hindu, and a conservative one at that.

The specifically Hindu element in the national movement had already been in evidence much earlier. Thus, in the first decade of the century when the British had proposed to partition Bengal, dividing it, as it later was divided, into a predominantly Muslim province and a predominantly Hindu one, the successful agitation for the abandonment of this plan was conducted by Hindus in specifically Hindu religious terms. (A left nationalist writer, J.M. Kaul, provides a typical instance of the presentation of what was in fact a Hindu movement in the acceptable national terms when he says that this movement showed 'the strength of the linguistic urge'.) (J.M. Kaul, *Problems of National Integration*, 1963, p.8.) So it did, but that was not all it showed.

Similarly, in the period of 1905–10 Tilak, the major leader of what was then called the extremist trend in Congress, campaigned against British rule by exalting the glories of ancient Hindu civilisation and rejecting everything (or in practice, somewhat less than everything) of 'imported' western culture.

Gandhi and the Muslim appeal

Gandhi achieved in the period 1918–22 the realisation of the aim of a united Hindu-Muslim mass movement against the British — the first, and indeed the only, time in recent Indian history where this aim was realised. But he achieved it by a wholesale acceptance of Muslim demands — which were essentially religious demands, completely utopian and completely reactionary.

The background to this calls for an (unfortunately rather lengthy) explanation. In the first two decades of the twentieth century Indian Muslims had been profoundly disturbed by European imperialist expansion at the expense of the Ottoman Empire, the last remaining Muslim empire. Though the British were not at first the prime movers in this expansion, Indian Muslims quite rightly thought that they supported those, like the French and the Italians, who were, and hostility to their British rulers grew apace. When after the end of the 1914–18 war Kemal Ataturk fought successfully to defeat the attempts of the British and their European allies to carve up Turkey into spheres of influence, Indian Muslims were delighted, and hailed him as a great hero. But their picture of what was happening was, and had been for decades, a totally false one. They had seen the Ottoman Empire as a great community of Muslim brethren, united in their reverence for their Emperor, whom they saw as not only a powerful ruler but as their Caliph, that is, as the spiritual guide of the world-wide Muslim community. When the Arabs during the war, urged on by the British and the French, threw off their allegiance to their Emperor-Caliph, Indian Muslims saw this as a shameful betrayal of their Muslim brothers. And when Kemal Ataturk appeared on the scene and went into battle against the British and their allies, they saw him as a holy warrior of Islam and a true servant of his Emperor-Caliph.

Nothing could have been further from the truth. Kemal had no interest in prolonging, or re-establishing, Turkish rule over the Arabs, and aimed to create a modern Turkey and break the hold of Muslim reactionaries over the Turkish people. In pursuit of this aim he attacked the caliphate, at first restricting the Caliph's powers and soon after abolishing the caliphate itself.

Meanwhile the Indian Muslims had launched a mass movement called the khilafat movement — khilafat is the Urdu word for caliphate — the object of which was to defend the caliphate against those who were out to destroy it. At that time Kemal had not yet moved against the caliphate, and the Indian Muslims were inspired by the entirely false picture just described. They thought that the British were out to destroy the caliphate, and it was the deep indignation against this supposed plan that moved them into action.

Gandhi was poised to launch a mass movement against the British authorities and against the extremely harsh steps, deeply resented by non-

Muslims and Muslims alike, which they were taking to crush all opposition. It would surely have been possible to form a principled alliance, to unite on a common platform to fight on the issues which united all Indians. But the Muslim masses were already on the move, and Gandhi chose instead to take, for the moment, the easier path of accepting the existing Muslim demands and persuading the Congress to accept them too.

Nationalist and Marxist interpretation

The treatment of this Muslim movement by nationalist (and Marxist) writers again illustrates the point which I made earlier. They attempt to show that the movement was in essence not a religious movement at all. Thus Nehru in his *Autobiography* (1936) p.69, wrote of the khilafat movement in an attempt to, so to speak, sanitise it, '...the word *khilafat* bore a strange meaning in most of the rural areas. People thought it came from "khilaf", an Urdu word meaning "against" or "opposed to" and so they took it to mean "opposed to Government"!' This is quite untrue. I once raised this question with Abdul Alim, a veteran Muslim communist and a friend of Nehru who had first come into political activity at the time of the khilafat movement. He told me that every Muslim knew perfectly well what khilafat meant.

A similar situation arose in the treatment of the Moplah rebellion in Kerala, which also took place at this time. The Moplahs were a Muslim community and their clash with the British authorities was indeed part of the national awakening of the period immediately following the First World War, but nationalist and communist writers alike present it solely in those terms, whereas in fact it had a militant anti-Hindu aspect as well and was accompanied by forcible conversion of Hindus to Islam. Nirad C. Chaudhuri in his book *Thy Hand, Great Anarch* (1987) — I cannot find the page reference — draws attention to a similar phenomenon in East Bengal. There, Muslim peasant attacks on landlords were always attacks on Hindu landlords; equally oppressive Muslim landlords were not attacked.

Indian nationalities

As I have already said, the freedom movement made an appeal also to the growing national consciousness in the various major linguistic regions of India, but this consciousness, much more pronounced in some regions than in others, was not a prominent feature of the pre-independence period. However, as early as 1927 the Indian National Congress passed a resolution in favour of the reorganisation of India into linguistic provinces. This stand was reiterated in October 1937, July 1938, and in the election manifesto of 1945–6. But national consciousness in this sense was not an important factor of the political scene before the Second World War.

The question of nationalities *within* India began to assume a somewhat greater importance during the Second World War. According to R. Palme Dutt, Stalin had already in 1912 given a friendly nod of approval of this development when he wrote 'in the case of India too, it will probably be found that innumerable nationalities, until then lying dormant, will come to life with the further course of bourgeois development'. (I had doubts about the attribution of this statement to 1912. My recollection was that it came a good deal later, and Monty Johnstone has kindly verified this for me. It comes in fact from an address of Stalin to the University of Toilers of the East made on 18 May 1925 — and the wording of the version in the Moscow 1954 edition of Stalin's works differs somewhat, though not very significantly, from that quoted by Dutt in *Labour Monthly*, March 1946 — subsequent quotations from Dutt are all from this article.)

The Communist Party of India in 1942 came to pay attention to this development, spurred on (and this is very significant) by the growing Muslim support for the demand for Pakistan. (I shall be returning to this point later.) R. Palme Dutt wrote of this:

> the report of G. Adhikari [a leading figure in the Communist Party of India] (republished in this country by *Labour Monthly* as a pamphlet under the title *Pakistan and National Unity*) brought out for the first time clearly the developing multi-national character of the India people, consequent on the wider mass extension of the national movement...and showed the political conclusions which must be drawn from this. 'Every section of the Indian people which has a contiguous territory as its homeland, common historical tradition, common language, culture, psychological make-up and common economic life would be recognised as a distinct nationality with the right to exist as an autonomous state within the free Indian Union or Federation and will have the right to secede from it if it may so desire.

National self-determination and the demand for Pakistan

The significance of the word 'Pakistan' in the title of the pamphlet stemmed, as I have indicated above, from the recognition that the Muslim League under its leader Jinnah now had mass support. It had in 1940 passed a resolution demanding the establishment of a separate political entity comprising the Muslim majority regions of North-West and East India which would be the homeland of what Jinnah called the Muslim nation. The resolution did not use the word Pakistan, but the demand soon came to be called the demand for Pakistan.

Faced with the fact that this demand now had mass backing, the Communist Party of India, characteristically, set itself the task of finding some sort of progressive content in it. It decided, on the basis of no evidence worth speaking of, that this was the distorted expression of the demand of the nationalities of those areas for self-determination. At this stage, in 1942, it appealed to the Muslim masses to drop the demand for Pakistan and reformulate it as a proper, acceptable demand for self-determination. But by 1944 it had moved to support for Pakistan, in the hope that it would be possible to bring about the interpretation of it that it wanted.

This whole interpretation was yet another case of a refusal to look at important facts that it didn't want to see. To those who did look at them it was clear even then that whatever the Pakistan demand expressed, it was not a demand, distorted or otherwise, for national self-determination put forward by the peoples of North-West and East India. Up to the very eve of the formation of Pakistan three years later, support for the Pakistan demand in the areas which came to constitute it was unimpressive. The most fervent supporters of Pakistan were, for reasons I will not go into, mainly to be found elsewhere, in regions which no one ever claimed would ever be part of Pakistan. But this did not stop the general secretary of the Communist Party of India declaring in 1944, 'The Pakistan demand is the demand of these [Muslim] nationalities for self-determination.' (Quoted by Dutt in the same article.) Dutt's purpose in writing his March 1946 article was to set the Indian communists to rights, which he did in his typically high-handed way, and they returned to their former stand of advocating self-determination for all the nationalities of India. (Let me remark in passing that later on, interviewed by journalists when he visited India, he brazenly denied that the communists had ever supported Pakistan, which, since everybody knew that this was a lie, cannot have done either him or the Indian communists much good.)

This led to a situation where on the eve of independence Congress was demanding a single constituent assembly to determine the future of independent India, the Muslim League was demanding two constituent assemblies, one for the Muslims and one for the rest, and the Communist Party was demanding seventeen. Such was the state of affairs when independence came in 1947.

Regional national movements after independence

It was only after the achievement of independence that the regional national movements gathered real strength, and now Congress performed a volte-face and took a stand against the formation of linguistic provinces — or, as they were now to be called (on the model of the USA), states. The background to this is understandable if not justifiable. The price paid for independence had been the partitioning of the country and the establishment of Pakistan, and Nehru and his associates were apprehensive about any movement which might result in the further break-up of independent India. Thus Nehru in a speech made on 2 October 1956 declared that 'the division of the country on the basis of language would be as harmful to India as the division of her people on the basis of religion or caste' (J.M. Kaul, op. cit. p. 18). However, Nehru and his colleagues were unable to resist the growing demand, and in fact Nehru had already suffered his first major defeat three years before this speech was made.

In Andhra a man named Potti Sriramalu began on 15 October 1952 a fast to the death for the immediate formation of an Andhra State, comprising the region whose people speak Telegu. (I should explain at this point that in India, while in some cases the names of a territory, its inhabitants and its language are much the same, this is often not the case. Thus Panjab is inhabited by Panjabis who speak Panjabi, but the language spoken by the people of Andhra is called Telegu. Similarly, Kerala is the name of a territory, the people of Kerala are called Malayalis, and their language is Malayalam.) Fasting to the death has been a common Indian political tactic and in general its purpose has been to force sufficient concessions to enable the fast to be called off without too much loss of face by either side. If the fast does in fact become a fast to the death, this precipitates a major crisis. And that is what happened in this case. Potti Sriramalu died after fifty-eight days of fasting. The demand for the establishment of Andhra Pradesh became irresistible, and on 19 December Nehru announced that it would be formed.

I shall not follow in detail the further development of the process of the formation of the linguistic provinces after the Andhra victory of December 1952. The other southern states — Tamilnadu, Karnataka and Kerala — were formed soon afterwards. Maharashtra and Gujarat were formed by 1960, and Panjab in 1966. In general the areas inhabited by aboriginal tribes were not granted statehood until later — Nagaland in 1963, Meghalaya in 1972, Arunachal Pradesh in 1987 and Mizoram also in 1987.

Paul Brass in his book *The Politics of India since Independence* (1990) speaks of the 'rules' operated by the central Indian leadership. These were, first, that no secession would be tolerated and that if necessary secessionist movements would be suppressed by force of arms. (The prolonged war against the Nagas was the clearest expression of this policy.) Second, there would be no concession to national demands if these were *communal* demands, i.e. the demands of a particular religious community. Thus it was not until the predominantly Sikh demand for a Panjabi linguistic province was presented in purely linguistic terms that the demand was finally granted. (The relatively early and problem-free formation of the linguistic states of Southern India was facilitated by the fact that, in general, tension between religious communities is much less pronounced than it is in the north. In the south the demand for linguistic states *was*, by and large, a purely national demand.) And third that there would be no recognition of 'nationalities' where mass national consciousness had not developed. (Brass quotes the example of the Maithili-speaking region of north Bihar. He says that Maithili can as properly be regarded as a language as Panjabi, but most Maithili speakers are content to see it as a dialect of Hindi and there is therefore no mass demand for the formation of a Maithili linguistic state.)

National consciousness, communal consciousness

The traditional communist and progressive analysis of these national movements has had a substantial measure of validity, but like most other areas of communist and progressive analysis it has been an insufficiently complex one. Thus if one looks at just a few of the national movements in India one can clearly see that very many of them, particularly in Northern India, have been almost as much communal movements as they have been national movements.

For example the Maharashtrian national movement goes back to at least the seventeenth century and it was indeed a movement to liberate from Mughal rule what one might loosely call the Maharashtrian nation. But it has been seen by Maharashtrians then and ever since as the revolt of a Hindu people against Muslim oppressors, and I think that Mahashtrian Muslims have felt no sympathy with it. In my unit in the Indian Army, I had a naik, (equivalent of corporal in the British Army), named Hamje Khan. I learnt that he came from what is now the state of Maharashtra and when I discovered this said to him 'Oh, then you're a Maratha.' 'No,' he said. 'I'm a Muslim' — a statement which clearly showed that he did not regard himself as belonging to the Maharashtrian 'nation' and that only the Hindus did. The great Maratha leader in the struggle against the Mughals was

Shivaji and it is significant that the viciously Hindu communal movement in contemporary Maharashtra calls itself the Shiv Sena, which means 'the Shiva army'. Another feature of the Maharashtrian national movement which has been in evidence from its earliest days has been the standard nationalist complete disregard of the rights of other nations. At the height of their power the Marathas invaded and levied tribute from regions extending over most of northern India and were rightly regarded by the peoples of these regions as oppressors.

The national movement of Bengal shows similar features. It developed in the nineteenth century and in the early days of the all-India national movement contributed much of the all-India leadership. Bengali nationalism too was an overwhelmingly Hindu nationalism. The British sold to Bengali Hindus the line that they had liberated them from Muslim rule, and throughout the greater part of the nineteenth century Bengali Hindus were markedly pro-British. This pro-British feeling eventually evaporated but widespread anti-Muslim bias remained and still remains. (To which it should be added that, as we have seen, Bengali Muslims similarly feel a strong anti-Hindu bias.) We have already seen how the campaign against the partition of Bengal in the first decade of the twentieth century was overwhelmingly Hindu-based. An English colleague of mine at the School of Oriental and African Studies who taught Bengali and spoke it extremely well told me that Bengalis often wondered whether he were a Bengali. Their first question to him would be 'Are you a Bengali?' and when he said that he was not, the second question would be 'Are you a Muslim?' as though 'Bengali' did not include 'Bengali Muslim'.

To this day the situation remains broadly the same, with Bengali Hindu exclusiveness paralleled by Bengali Muslim exclusiveness. When East Pakistan (as it then was) broke away from Pakistan and formed itself into the independent state of Bangladesh there was indeed an upsurge there of Bengali consciousness, and much talk of glorious Bengali traditions. In a talk I gave at the time I stressed that it was an independent *Muslim* state that was being formed. A woman in the audience just back from Bangladesh came up to me afterwards and said, 'They are not talking in those terms: they speak of Bengal.' I said, 'Yes, but have you heard *any* of them saying that we can now unite the Indian state of West Bengal with our new state and form a united Bengal?' 'Well, no,' she said. 'No,' I said, 'you wouldn't have.'

In Panjab the situation is somewhat different, but Panjabi national feeling has always been expressed predominantly by the Sikhs of the Panjab, and Panjabi Hindus and Panjabi Muslims have been very little affected by it. Thus it is only the Sikhs who have for generations now classed Panjabi as a literary language. Hindus and Muslims have commonly regarded it as a sort of 'kitchen and household' language and nothing more, and class it respectively as a dialect of Hindi or a dialect of Urdu.

There are remarkable expressions of this attitude. Thus Prakash Tandon, a highly educated Panjabi Hindu who attained the distinction of becoming the first Indian chairman of Hindustan Lever, writes in the first volume of his autobiography *(Punjabi Century,* 1961, Hind Pocket Books paperback edition, p.66) 'Our language, Punjabi, has no script.' (He uses the traditional spelling Punjab, Punjabi rather than the more accurate spelling with an 'a'.) By this he really means, 'We Panjabi Hindus don't write Panjabi'. He knows perfectly well that the Sikhs do write Panjabi and have a distinctive Panjabi script for it.

On the other side of the communal divide is a similar instance of this kind of feeling. A friend of mine who visited Indian Panjab came back with a piece of embroidered material on which something was written which she could not read. She showed it to a Panjabi Muslim friend of hers and said 'Can you read this? I presume it's in Panjabi.' He replied, 'Oh, it can't be in Panjabi. Panjabi can't be written.'

This reminds me of the dictum of Max Weinreicht, 'A language is a dialect that has an army and a navy'. Only the Sikhs have provided Panjabi with 'an army and a navy' and therefore it is only for them that Panjabi is a language. I wrote earlier something which suggested that the demand for a Panjabi linguistic province was essentially a Sikh demand and was originally presented as such. It continued to be a predominantly Sikh demand, but the Sikh leaders eventually had the sense to present it in linguistic terms and thus enable the central government to grant the demand without obviously breaking one of its 'rules' as Paul Brass calls them.

Just to conclude, I wrote earlier of nationalities' disregard of the rights of other nationalities and quoted the early example of the Marathas. This feature has been evident too in post-independence India. Thus some of the Andhra leaders who campaigned for the formation of Andhra state demanded that it include Madras, which is overwhelmingly not a Telegu-speaking, but a Tamil-speaking city and was quite rightly included in Tamilnadu when that state was formed. Similarly in Assam there are large minorities of Bengalis and of tribal peoples and the Assamese nationalists have been very markedly hostile to the rights of both.

A final note on nationalism: it is significant of the power of the appeal of the concept of national self-determination that purely communal movements have often described themselves as national movements, thus conferring on themselves a respectability they would otherwise lack. Thus the Muslim League demand for Pakistan was always presented as a demand for a homeland for the Muslim *nation* and the militant Hindu communal movements in India today insist that India is a Hindu *nation*, and that if you're not a Hindu you're not an Indian. However, this ploy does not do much to disguise the real nature of these movements.

Kashmir

I have not said anything hitherto about the problem of Kashmir. This is because, like everyone else, I have seen this as mainly a problem of international relations between India and Pakistan. However, it is relevant to say something about it here. One must start by saying that the Kashmir problem has not been seen by anybody as predominantly a problem of national self-determination for the Kashmiri people. By and large, there are good reasons for this. When India became independent in 1947 Indian territory was a jumble of British-ruled provinces and princely states ruled by native rulers under British paramountcy, and the boundaries of neither bore much relevance to the boundaries of linguistic areas. When the two new dominions of India and Pakistan were formed, it was agreed that the rulers of these states could if they wished accede either to the Indian Union or to Pakistan. Kashmir was a state with a predominantly Muslim population ruled by a Hindu prince and its accession to India took the form of a decision by this prince, backed by Indian armed force, to accede to India. Since it was a predominantly Muslim state, Pakistan argued (probably correctly) that the wishes of the Kashmiri population would be that it should accede to Pakistan, and they invaded Kashmir in order to enforce this decision. Eventually a ceasefire was agreed under United Nations auspices and the United Nations recommended that a plebiscite should be held to decide the question — i.e. to decide whether the state should accede to India or to Pakistan. The Indian government accepted this recommendation but later went back on it.

In the course of time it was suggested that the people of Kashmir should have a third option, namely to choose to be a state independent of both India and Pakistan. But when one comes to consider this third option one is faced with the fact that the state, which to give it its full title, is the State of Jammu and Kashmir, is one which was historically formed on the basis of the conquest of both Jammu and Kashmir by the Sikh kingdom of the Panjab in the early part of the nineteenth century, and would seem to have no greater linguistic justification as a unit than the similarly formed

British provinces and princely states of pre-independence India. If one is to be consistent in advocating self-determination one would have to recognise that Jammu and Kashmir is not the territory of a single nationality. The Kashmir Valley in which Srinagar, the major city of Kashmir, is situated is populated by Kashmiri-speaking Muslims. In Jammu, the people are Dogri-speaking Hindus, and in yet another region, that of Ladakh, one could argue that there is yet another distinct nationality. Thus both Pakistan's demand that the whole state should accede to Pakistan and India's demand that the whole state should accede to India is not quite the same as a principled demand for national self-determination. However, these questions are not likely in the foreseeable future to be ones which have much bearing on practical politics.

What conclusions should we draw?

When one surveys all these questions of Indian nationality, one should not be led to conclude that there was no validity in the analysis made by communists and Indian progressives such as Nehru. There was, but as I indicated earlier, it presented, like many other Marxist-Leninist analyses, a simple picture of what was in fact a complex situation. This analysis presumed that in the short or middle term class consciousness would prevail over religious and nationalist consciousness, and clearly, not only has this not happened, there is no short- or middle-term — perhaps not even any long-term — prospect of it happening. Which of course does not mean that Marxists and communists should not continue to exert themselves to help all movement in that direction. That they cannot do more than that is no reason for not doing it.

Aliens and Little Britons

Anna Davin

My parents were New Zealanders and I think that gives me a sense of how people can have more than one national identity at once or how the relationship between different parts of your background helps to shape the person you are and the way you place yourself socially and politically. That is really what lies behind this article; it is loosely based on the last chapter of my book but there are overlaps and differences....The book is about working class children in late nineteenth and early twentieth century London which is why it is called *Growing Up Poor*: most of them were. In the book I particularly look at gender differences and at the impact of compulsory school on experiences of childhood.

When I started working on that book (which took me, I may say, 25 years — I'm not a very fast worker) as I started off it was at the beginning of social history and History Workshop, and we were thinking of new areas that were important like the family as well as work, unwaged work as well as paid work; childhood as well as adults; gender. We were looking at anthropology for interesting ways of approaching history and some of that comes across in my work, for instance, when I talk about children's games. But I think it is also there in my sense of the relationships between children; both anthropology and sociology feed into what I'm doing with history. Very often, partly because of academic pressures and the way that research and writing are organised, people tend to take one approach or one subject matter and get quite blinkered about it. I was always trying not to do that, which is partly why it took me so long. I wanted to write in this book on childhood about questions of national identity, culture, ethnic and religious culture, to integrate those issues too.

The history of the family often assumes there is only one homogenous British family; it might be divided by class and region but basically there is said to be a family there that is going to be much the same give or take a few differences like that. Unlike in American social history there has not been much attention to the kinds of difference that relate to the family's religion, to its politics, to its possible use of more than one language, to its possibly being first or second generation from somewhere else. Similarly when people look at London they don't think that much about where people came from before London; even though London has been continually remade for its entire span of existence and it has always been made by people coming in. Even when it wasn't actually growing — which a lot of the time it was — people were dying at a higher rate because it was such an unhealthy place and so incomers were topping it up. But a lot of the time and certainly in the period I've been looking at it was also growing very fast and that growth was not what is called the natural growth with more babies being born, because although they were a great many of them were also dying. Most of its growth was people coming in; they were coming in from the Home Counties and the rest of England and the rest of the British Isles, from Europe and particularly, of course, in the late nineteenth century from eastern Europe and also even from across the Atlantic and from other parts of the empire.

There was a Museum of London exhibition called 'Londoners From Everywhere' a while back; I taught a course called that ten years before they put it on and I was very pleased that they had taken that title because the way in which Londoners do come from everywhere and bring so much in the way of different social, cultural and economic experience and skills with them has been a very important part of why London is such a dynamic and interesting place, whether you are talking culturally, politically, economically or whatever. But it is also a source of complexity, contest and conflict within the city. How those differences work themselves out in neighbourhoods, on the street, in the workplace, even in the family is a very interesting thing to explore.

The explanations of cultural identity (which has been much more studied in the last ten to fifteen years) have tended to be in terms of the things that you can get at most easily, like what was happening in the music hall, popular literature, newspapers. You can for example read newspapers and see the caricatures as paradigms of ethnic identities and the way in which assumptions are being made about this group or that group and hostility or approval expressed. There has been a fair amount of this work, looking at the racist underpinnings of schoolbooks for instance and relating those to the empire; for example John MacKenzie's book, *Propaganda and Empire; the manipulation of British public opinion, 1880 to 1960*. I like that span: it reminds us that although my research is pre-First World War: its themes are of course incredibly relevant in the whole of the twentieth century.

MacKenzie looks at theatre, cinema, radio, imperial exhibitions, the Imperial Institute, imperial propaganda societies and imperial studies, imperialism and the school textbook, imperialism and juvenile literature, imperial propaganda and extracurricular activities. He really documents the extent to which imperialist ideas and thinking dominated or infiltrated the general culture in the late nineteenth and early twentieth centuries.

A more recent book, Cathy Castle's *Britannia's Children: Reading colonialism through children's books and magazines,* does something of the same kind but in a kind of ten, fifteen years later way, asking slightly different questions of the same material and doing more theorising; it is a very interesting and useful book as well.

The most recent theoretical approach, which brings in psychoanalysis, is Graham Dawson's *Soldier Heroes: British Adventure, Empire and the Imagining of Masculinities*; I think this is a really exciting book but if you find theory heavygoing you should skip the first few chapters — as the author does himself advise. It has chapter titles like 'Soldier Heroes and the Narrative Imagining of Masculinities,' 'Masculinity, Fantasy and History,' 'The Adventure Question and its Cultural Imaginaries' and 'The Imagining of a Hero: Sir Henry Havelock, the Indian Rebellion and the News.' The Havelock chapter looks at the creation of a hero in the colonial wars of the mid-nineteenth century in India and relates it to the development of the wireless telegraph and how fast the news was now coming in. Everything becomes much more immediate and people hang on it; we can see similar things happening with television news in our generation. He looks at the way that Havelock gets made into a kind of imperial saint. Then he takes Lawrence of Arabia and looks at the history of who he was and what he did and again the turning of him into another kind of imperial saint. Subsequently he looks at his own childhood and the influences on that and the games that he remembers playing, the people that he remembers imagining he was, in chapters called 'Playing at Soldiers; Boyhood Fantasies and the Pleasure Culture of War' and 'Self-Imagining: Boyhood Masculinity, Social Recognition and the Adventure Hero.'

So these are the new buzzwords and phrases and they relate to a new set of questions about fantasy, about psychoanalysis, about the construction of the self, about how you make yourself and about what else goes into the shaping of 'you' in a quite internal way; but he is trying to relate it to outside influences and social and economic and political contexts in a way I find really interesting. I could not possibly do it myself, but it is quite exciting.

Imperial culture

I have made the point that imperial ideas dominated popular culture in the late nineteenth and early twentieth century. When I say imperial I am also thinking of militarist and racist and a very gendered, masculinist set of ideas and ways of thinking. They dominated what was available to read, whether the quality press or the popular press or books and articles. They dominated what you might hear, from the music hall to Elgar. They dominated toys: this is the highpoint of lead toy soldiers for instance and of nurse costumes, the girls' equivalent of the soldier in this context. It is the period when you have jigsaw puzzles and maps of the world with a lot of bits painted red and also during the war with bits painted blue which are the enemy. All those kinds of ideas are being reiterated in the classroom, in the church, in the pub, in the cornershop and on the street corner. Really they are everywhere. But in the discussion at the level of the quality press and the House of Commons and the classes that had control over things in this period the influence of the Boer War is very important. During the Boer War we have the mighty English military machine and imperial administration tied up in a war with a tiny people, really very few in numbers compared with the British might, who for three years managed to hang in there. It is only marginally a British victory, only just, a pretty pyrrhic victory; a lot of people were lost, a lot of money was spent, they only just held onto the prestige of managing to win. It also caused a lot of divisions domestically, as did the last Gulf War.

That experience focused attention on the production of soldiers; the maintenance of Britain as an imperial and military society. It focused attention — as I wrote a long time ago in an article about imperialism and motherhood — on the conditions of producing and rearing children. But it also focused attention on how children were being educated. Since the Education Act of 1870 there had been a spreading network of state schools very much geared towards civilising the natives of England, the poor or uncivilised as they were perceived. Teaching them was not just about reading and writing and arithmetic but all sorts of things about how they ought to behave, how to be British and what their wonderful Anglo-Saxon heritage was and how fortunate they were to be part of this mighty empire; what a privileged future they had as soldiers, nurses or mothers of our boys. You have all of that going on in the schools as well as outside. They were told that they were in possession of an empire, the greatest, for which no sacrifice was too great. You can see how this ethic was building up to the chauvinism of the First World War and how unquestioningly young men went off to war and families sent them in many cases just to be slaughtered; all was absolutely within this way of thinking.

This question of mothers and empire also ties in with the position of Britain and Queen Victoria; she was the mother of empire, England was the mother country, the dominions were like older sons, they were white-settled, and the colonies which were administered by white colonials but had black majority populations, were like wayward children and needed white adult authority to get anywhere and learn their place in the world. So assumptions of a hierarchy in the family then metaphorically get extended to the empire — there are often connections like that which you see very easily when you think of them, indeed it is totally obvious.

It is also very obvious that there is a strong racist and eugenic component in all of this. The typical Englishman of the past who is constantly alluded to is first of all an English *man*, second he is always fair and blue eyed, there are constant references to Anglo-Saxon heritage. Derogatory references to Irish and Jews are very common. There is also and interestingly because of the eugenic influence a lot of stress on having a sound physique; it is in the 1890s and 1900s that we begin to see schoolchildren who have disabilities separated out into special schools — which in some ways was good because it gave them special attention rather than have them simply falling behind and being ignored — but in other ways was bad because it started a labelling process which culminated in the 1913 Mental Defectives Act. The assumption was that if you are not of sound mental and physical being then you can't be a citizen and you may have to be locked in an institution for your whole life and segregated. That Mental Defectives Act also had a provision whereby somebody who was seen as morally defective could be incarcerated and in the last twenty years or so we have seen examples of people in their eighties being released who had been locked up in their teens for promiscuity or for having a child outside wedlock or for having a relationship with somebody of the same sex or a different race. So what was 'defective' had a horrendously wide range of definitions.

The ethnic mix

It is one thing to have all this nice tidy ideology about an Anglo-Saxon past and a perfect population but in real life a great many London children were not of Anglo-Saxon stock and might not have a drop of Anglo-Saxon blood in them. The ideology completely leaves out all the people of mixed 'stock' (the word of the day and not one I like very much). This makes it very difficult to work out statistics for the period, which is one of the problems in trying to work out how many children were what, even leaving out all the people who were second generation or who were mixed. I think that of about 500,000 children in late nineteenth century London who were of school age probably about 30,000 were Irish first generation, but there would have been a lot more who were second and third generation. Probably about over 10,000 were Jewish, but it isn't very easy because the school records are not kept that way and the census isn't kept that way. You have to rely on people's estimates at the time, which vary.

Then of course there were enclaves of other nationalities like the old Italian quarter west of the Fleet river (now Farringdon Road). As you go up the hill you can still see an Italian church, and an Italian driving school, and there is still an Italian delicatessen in the market street. There are still people with Italian names around there I would guess. It used to be the ice-cream capital of London as well; ice cream barrows came out from Clerkenwell to travel all over London. The other major Italian occupation seems to have been making plaster figures of the sort that go in gardens or on walls, window sills or in churches. So we have enclaves like this, or like the German sugar bakers in the outer east end. Then there were very mixed neighbourhoods like Soho and parts of the east end closer to the river with lots of different nationalities co-existing. Then the enormous Jewish population of Spitalfields, Bethnal Green, Stepney and shading out into the surrounding areas as well. Spitalfields being just north of the early port area of London has a history of one wave after another of newcomers. In the late nineteenth century the latest comers were Jewish; they joined a very strong Irish population which overlaid a Huguenot and English population. So it was mixed but most visibly Jewish, and reflecting that there were several all-Jewish schools. In the rest of London the Jewish population was more scattered and there would not be special Jewish schools. With Irish children also there were concentrations in the east end, around Covent Garden and central places and concentrations in inner West London. In all of these places you find Catholic churches and Catholic church schools, although often they were not enough for the population. There were also plenty of Irish people scattered in many other parts of London with certainly not enough churches or schools; in these places the Irish children attended the regular board schools. So the board schools almost always had some Irish and some Jewish children, but the more strongly Irish or Jewish a neighbourhood was the more likely it was that there would be schools that were predominantly Irish or Jewish. This is tied up with what religious provision there was as well.

Poor Jewish and Irish children lived in much the same conditions as other local children usually and the same would be true of smaller and less concentrated minorities; in some ways being poor was what determined your experience and not what your ethnic or religious background was. But at the same time they were different. On the one hand that was true through their sense of identity, which was being created at home, in the community if there was enough of them to constitute a local community, perhaps in their religion, so there is a way in which their sense of identity was coming from being part of something, being part of an Irish or Jewish family or community or being Catholic or Jewish in religion. On the other hand a sense of identity was also being created because they were perceived and treated as different by some of their peers and by the schools. So there was an internal construction of difference and an imposed construction. In this way their experience both overlapped with and differed from that of other poor children. In school English was enforced and assimilation was encouraged; foreign parents and children were not put at their ease. There is a good example of this from the life of the Jewish painter Mark Gertler who grew up in Spitalfields. When he first went to school his Yiddish speaking mother in her anxiety picked him up as they stood in the queue to register even though he was already seven and quite heavy. The story goes:

> ...at last our turn came to approach the desk, at which a man was sitting, very stern and angry, making us feel from the start that we were in the wrong, and that he jolly well meant to let us have it. 'Put that boy down *at once*. He is not a babe! Name of Gertler, I see. What's his Christian name?' [Which is of course an absurd question and a meaningless one.] Of course my mother could make nothing of it at all until some woman at the back came to the rescue. 'Mux', she said. 'Mux?' said the man, 'Never heard of such a name — no such name in this country — we'll call him *Mark* Gertler', and nodding to a woman nearby and pointing his pen he said 'Next'.

You get there the cultural absurdity of a Jewish mother being asked what her son's Christian name is and of course not understanding. And then the accent of the woman who stepped in to help meant that the registrar could not hear the name 'Max' and instead substituted the name 'Mark'; there must have been just countless examples of that kind of thing.

On starting school many children had to learn English for the first time and become bilingual. Ena Abrahams remembered the local cinema to which Yiddish-speaking mothers and grandmothers took children in the

1920s as 'terribly noisy because we all used to do simultaneous translation.' Some succumbed to school influences as their English improved and especially if there were no grandparents around, and gave up on their first language. Ruth Adler's teacher in 1920s Stepney said 'If you want to learn English, you must speak English, read English and dream in English.' Her father roared with laughter on hearing this but she stopped speaking Yiddish nevertheless. Her parents for a time answered her English with Yiddish but eventually they too spoke English. (This is from a lovely book called *A Family of Shopkeepers*, an autobiographical novel by Ruth Adler which I found in paperback in the mid-1970s. I don't think it has been reprinted, but it is worth looking out for.) As the writer observed this abandoning of your first language in childhood once you went to school was a very common story, and not only among Jews. Irish children did not always come from Irish speaking areas. Those who did might not retain knowledge of the language and those born in London might never learn it, so this process did not necessarily apply as strongly to them as it did to Jewish children. In retrospect adults often regret not having maintained their mother tongue: 'If you are made to feel that your language is second rate — it does something to your self-image which it probably takes you the better part of your lifetime to recover from.'

Manufacturing Britishness

In the last decades of the nineteenth century the term 'alien', which basically meant Jew, was used to focus xenophobia in a vociferous campaign for the restriction of immigration, which resulted in the 1905 Aliens Act. Even writers who opposed immigration control assumed that there was a problem for which Anglicisation was the answer and might lapse into using stereotypes. So you have the ones who were saying 'get rid of them, kick them out' or 'don't let any more in' and the others who said 'well it's all right to let them in but they have got to learn to be English.' Children were exposed to these ideas both from the general culture and their specific experiences. In London board schools most teachers had been through training colleges where admission was conditional on being a practising Christian. I've found the odd letter from fathers saying, 'I really want my daughter to be a teacher and she wants to have the proper training at your college but we can't send the required certificate of confirmation because we are not Church of England: they were Jewish or atheist or simply nonconformists. There were a number of places where this was a problem. If you had not been confirmed it was much harder for you to obtain formal training to become a teacher. You could teach as an uncertificated teacher but you were paid less and would not win promotion. Teachers from the colleges had often been raised to believe in British superiority, although some resisted attempts at the turn of the century to bring racist and imperialist politics into the classroom. However, I suspect the majority did not. There was one particularly venomous teacher, so patriotic that she wore a union jack apron. In the predominantly Jewish Commercial Street school in 1905, two years after the 1903 pogroms and in the year of the Aliens Act, she told the class:

> 'Now all you foreigners who come from Russia — you should all go back to your own country!' And a girl sitting in the front — her name was Yetta Solomons — she was so incensed about that...she took out this ink well and flung it at her, and she smashed her glasses...and all the ink ran down her. I always remember that.

Textbooks and teachers' books regularly presented Anglocentric images and information. They took for granted that Britons, Anglo-Saxons, deserved their empire. 'It was assumed', comments one historian, 'that all the subject peoples welcomed the peace and order of the British rule and that it was the duty rather than the pleasure of British people to carry out the task of maintaining the empire....' The relative standing of each subordinate country depended on its usefulness to Britain. Agricultural production, transport and industry all happened magically with no mention of labour unless in terms of native indolence and inefficiency. Following the pseudo-scientific racism developed over the previous century, the peoples of the empire were ranked in a hierarchy of race based mainly on skin colour. The original inhabitants of India, for instance, were 'a dark-skinned race who had to give way to people of fairer type and superior intellect and knowledge'. Of course you had the same picture of the British Isles, with the dark Celts relegated to the Celtic fringe and the Anglo-Saxons followed by the Normans who were sometimes fair as well as dark. In the popular application of Darwin's theories white skin and Anglo-Saxon civilisation were seen as the culmination of the evolutionary process.

The cumulative effect of lessons and stories which celebrated England's past could be powerful, according to the Jewish writer Israel Zangwill in his *Children of the Ghetto* of 1892. It is a wonderful account of ghetto life and the assimilation of a young up and coming intellectual; in this partly autobiographical novel eleven year old Esther Ansell spoke Yiddish at home but

> ...she led a double life just as she spoke two tongues....The knowledge that she was a Jewish child, whose people had a special history, was always at the back of her consciousness; sometimes it was brought to the front by the scoffing rhymes of English children, who informed her that they had stuck a piece of pork on a fork and given it to a member of her race. But far more vividly did she realise that she was an English girl; far keener than her pride in Judas Maccabaeus was her pride in Nelson and Wellington; she rejoiced to find that her ancestors had always beaten the French, from the days of Crecy and Poitiers to the day of Waterloo; that Alfred the Great was the wisest of kings, and that English men dominated the world and had planted colonies in every corner of it; that the English language was the noblest in the world, and men speaking it had invented railway trains, steamships, telegraphs, and everything worth inventing. Esther absorbed these ideas from the school textbooks.

I like this book because of the double perspective. She is feeling both her Jewish identity and also getting a very strong English sense.

The Empire Day movement of the 1900s encouraged schools to celebrate Britain's imperial achievements. Interestingly it did allow for some difference: not Jewish, but Welsh, Scottish, Irish and sometimes dominion difference. Union Jacks were distributed, there were displays of drill by the boys, the pupils joined in tableaux and processions in which the countries of the empire were represented by costumed pupils. National songs were sung and finally the whole school would be joined by watching parents, all singing:

> What is the meaning of empire?
> Why does the cannon roar?
> Why does the cry 'God Save the King'
> Echo from shore to shore?

In these performances Britannia presided over the scene and would be played by a tall child, probaby fair skinned, with strict instructions as to how it should be done. Different countries were represented by contingents of children in appropriate costume and if possible looks. That sort of occasion needed preparation and the whole school built up to it. A lot of the preparations and the performance were fun; it was not imposed but felt like a real break from everyday boring school. Similarly some of the lightweight educational material that was used for recitations and performances to encourage elocution and develop the memory presented images, for example, of a happy child-like negro; in some of them you find 'Sambo', Aunt Eliza, 'darkies' and so on. Ostensibly sympathetic they imply white and British superiority by trivialising and patronising the other peoples. Racist stereotypes abounded in children's books and comics, which were of course burgeoning in this period with cheaper print, cheaper techniques and paper, better distribution and slightly more disposable income (at least some children could afford to buy penny comics) and penetration of the working class market through the popular press that extended even to children. In all of this we constantly have stories of fair skinned heroes endlessly defeating ruffians of every shade of colour. Black people are savages and just like children; Britons the wise adults. We have aliens who are in all sorts of different ways the villains.

Autobiographical material from London and elsewhere suggests that newcomers were often seen and treated differently both at school and in the neighbourhood, especially of course if they were few and if culture and language reinforced difference. The exact character of the neighbourhood mattered, whether one group predominated, how much of a mix or what particular mix there was, and the rate of turnover. In a very mixed neighbourhood a degree of tolerance was probably necessary.

Stigma and intolerance

Louis Heren, who wrote an autobiography about growing up in Shadwell in the 1920s (and who became a well-known journalist on *The Times*), writes about how there was a complex combination of race and religion, but he says 'prejudice never led to physical violence', although I don't take his recollection of this as gospel. Everyone 'except possibly the non-conformists' celebrated St Patrick's Day and the young Heren, though a Protestant, wore a shamrock to school.

> The native-born Cockneys were certainly a minority, and the majority were immigrants, mainly Irish Catholics and Polish Jews. Some African and West Indian seamen had married local women and settled down. One of the...lodging houses was home for Indian pedlars, Sikhs who hawked garish scarves and shawls....There was no racial violence but religious prejudice was intense throughout the neighbourhood. I suppose we were all anti-semitic because we knew that the Jews had killed Jesus. Many of our Jewish neighbours spoke only Polish and Yiddish. The beards and the sidecurls of the orthodox

> were absolutely foreign. Apart from the Jews, the mutual antipathies of the Catholics and Protestants were constant, and the Nonconformists hardly ever spoke to anyone....Yet we all lived peacefully alongside each other if not together. We were all poor.

There is a real tension in that account; the differences are strong, there are conflicts and yet he is choosing to emphasise the poverty over the differences. I think they are probably both true.

Political and economic contexts interact with stereotypes to produce a specific local impact. When a particular group was perceived as flooding in and affecting wage rates, rents and conditions, hostility was intense. Anti-Irish sentiment, although this also fluctuated with the level of Fenian activity, was therefore strongest in the middle decades of the nineteenth century, when we have the biggest influx following the famine years and British economic development was demanding more and more Irish labour. For instance, Tom Barclay, in his autobiography subtitled *Memoirs of a Bottlewasher* recalls how in 1860s Leicester children echoed their parents' animosity, jeering at the newcomers' speech and generally abusing them. He describes the children as imitating Irish language in order to insult the Irish. 'These were the salutes from the happy English child: we were battered, threatened, elbowed, pressed back to the door of our kennel amid boos and jeers and showers of small missiles.'

By the 1890s, especially in London, antagonism was directed at newer arrivals. Walter Southgate recalled of his Hackney childhood how he and his friends made 'an old Jewish gentleman' in prosperous Gore Road their butt.

> Why, I don't know, but no boy could pass this old man's house without kicking on his door, ringing his bell, throwing stones at his gate and occasionally breaking his windows....It had become a ritual. There was no rhyme or reason for it except he was a Jew and they had invaded the East End as had other races in the past and were exploited by their compatriots, cheapening their labour products to the detriment of the East End English cabinetmakers.

He has a class interpretation of internal divisions in the Jewish population which a lot of others would not have had; as a relatively radical character he is recalling a childhood that he is not very proud of being a part of.

In each case current fears and prejudice provided substance for taunts and identified victims both for ordinary mischief and for more serious bullying and aggression. What I am saying here is that children always find reasons for hostility, if they are not getting on with each other they taunt each other. If they are getting on with each other they ignore the differences. Visible differences of language, of religion, of ethnicity, of dress and culture were very easy things to pick up on, to form gangs on, to make victims out of. They could be an excuse for gang rivalry and territoriality, especially among boys. Tom Barclay, again in 1860s Leicester, noted dispassionately that local boys' hostility was not only against the Irish, 'Sassenach kids fought amongst themselves. Street fought street and district district without the slightest cause.' Or in mid-century Clerkenwell small boys and lads, Catholic Irish and 'patriot' Italians (that is nationalist followers of Garibaldi who were anti-Catholic) fought in endless scrimmages for Garibaldi or the Pope; their form of cowboys and Indians. In South Hackney in the 1890s boys from Sidney Street board school fought boys from the free Catholic school down the road, to the dismay of an eleven year old girl whose route home lay through the battlefield. (This woman, born in 1882, whom I taped in the early 1970s, said to me. 'And if you can show me any more horrible little roughs than Irish Roman Catholics....') It is likely that the sons of the Wapping Irish saw Whitechapel Jewish boys as the enemy.

The victims of predatory or bullying behaviour were not always of another background of course, but such difference was one possible 'justification'. Whatever the pretext many individual children — girls and boys — were picked on by street bullies, as was Rose Kerrigan in Glasgow before the First World War for being Jewish:

> We were waylaid quite often coming home from the Hebrew school, especially on winter nights. My mother hid in a doorway one night when we were coming home. We had come home crying because these boys had hit us, we were running from them. My mother came out with an umbrella and gave them such a fright they never came back.

Adults as well as children might be the butt of taunts or worse because their appearance marked them out. Just as jeers and perhaps stones might greet an obvious nob, a missionary or a school board officer, so too an obvious identity as Jewish especially one newly arrived or with very orthodox dress, or someone obviously Irish or otherwise foreign might trigger hostility. Going back to a point I began with, children's own sense of difference would stem from both internal sources (how their household lived, its history, its religion, its consciousness) and from external ones, neighbourhood and school responses. And these interacted: Tom Barclay under attack in Leicester combined contempt and hatred for 'the Sassenach' with awareness of historical context and a certain pride in being Irish. As his mother said, 'Ah well sure what better could one expect of the breed of King Harry.' When he and his younger siblings were literally besieged in their hovel, he thought of the siege of Limerick. They deliberately identified with the heroes of Limerick so as not to get too scared while waiting for their parents. And Zangwill's Esther, as we have seen, 'knew herself as Jewish but still more vividly realised that she was an English girl'. I think it was especially difficult if you were from a smaller minority group without a community around for solidarity; for instance children of African, Caribbean, Indian or Chinese origin might be isolated in this kind of way and also had to contend with images which denigrated them as savages, dirty, uncivilised, childlike, devious, cunning and all the other images that were prevalent. Also names based on racial or national origin and alleged attributes like 'chink' were used by other children to taunt just as cries of Jew or Paddy were commonplace. If a girl had her hair done in one long plait, the boys would come and try to have a swing on it and shout 'there goes a Chinaman'. The woman I taped born in 1882 in Poplar told me how they used to creep up behind Chinese men with their long pigtails and dare each other to pull it and run away. There was a real presence of the Chinese pigtail in the late nineteenth century; it was not just an image in comics. (It is interesting the way that racist taunt was combined with the little boys' delight in teasing girls by pulling their plaits.) Then where one parent was English and the other of one of these ethnic groups there was the added stigma of being mixed.

The state and integration

There can be no doubt that East End children whose physical appearance suggested foreign parentage were sometimes made to feel different or even inferior whether at best by being patronised or by being ridiculed, teased, insulted or bullied. That this could happen in school as well as out and that it could come from adults, teachers included, as well as from children can be enlarged to conclude that the school was playing a part not only in redefining childhood but also playing a central part in the construction of national identity. What was further happening was that 'normal' childhood was being created in this period, when the concentration of children into schools made it much more possible to monitor and define what was normal and what was not; for instance, what was the right height for children of each age, what a healthy child should look like, who fell below the norm — and some fell so far below the norm that they needed to be segregated off into other kinds of institutions. All of this went with a rhetoric of the state as parent and an extension of the metaphor of the family. The state was beginning to be not only *in loco parentis* with orphans where the parents had gone, but increasingly it was challenging parents' rights. Protective legislation meant that children didn't do paid labour to anything like the old extent; the authorities now determined how children should be educated, the state would provide education but parents had to do as the state said and go along with it. There was even state intervention in issues of how children were reared.

I am not passing judgement on whether these interventions by the state were good or bad; what I am saying is that they were happening and the balance of power between parents and the state was changing. Parents — especially if they were poor, foreign or if their English was not very good, if they were not C of E, or if they did not go along with the dominant militarist and imperialist ideas — were more likely to be overruled in various ways. It was perhaps a paternalist state but in taking on parental responsibilities was also also infantilising real parents. The family metaphor which I suggested was applied to the empire was also applied internally in class terms: the working class were not seen as full adults. Many of them still did not have the vote, particularly women, so in political terms they were not full citizens, but in a whole lot of other ways the state was overriding them. The school played a part in all of this; the future British people needed to learn their place in the nation and the world in a complex interplay of class and gender and culture. The acknowledged objective of the school was to integrate and civilise children of the poor and Anglicise foreign children to ensure that the next generation met the needs of the modern nation state. Charles Russell, a Toynbee Hall Church of England worker, wrote in 1900: 'The newly arrived Russo-Jewish immigrant is in all essentials a medieval product, but his children grow up into something like the type of modern Englishman.' The Jewish Free School was praised by a reporter in 1895 as: 'A factory of English citizens' and he recounted his amazement in finding that of the hundred or so teachers engaged in turning these little foreigners into English folk only one, not all as he had supposed, was English and presumably Christian.

Israel Zangwill was more critical of the process of integration. In *The Children of the Ghetto* he wrote of the children of every country and kind who came 'from the reeking courts and alleys, from the garrets and the cellars' to be Anglicised, 'all hastening at the inexorable clang of the big school bell to be ground in the same great, blind, inexorable Governmental machine.' Zangwill refused to identify with a perception common to the Anglo-Jewish establishment and liberal middle class that anglicisation was necessary. As he saw, the school in this period played a central part in the consolidation of modern national identity. Although there were some who learned their lesson imperfectly or who rejected it or were themselves were rejected as misfits, board school children were being taught to be British.

Finally, it is too easy to assume that because you can show all of these things happening they had a general and uniform impact, it is like saying there is violence on television therefore all children are violent. There is racism in the dominant culture but we cannot assume that everyone exposed to it comes out racist, still less when they are themselves part of the minorities who are the objects of racism. I think that the strength of the left in the East End and the internationalism of the movement which we can see [in Spanish Civil War] posters around us here now and which is embodied in the building we are in, is an important reminder that some people did react to racism in another way. It is possible to work for internationalism, peace and ways to encompass plural identities and one international identity without repressing or imposing. That is still my ideal, if the conflicts I have been describing are still with us, we must remember the tradition that resisted them. Also remember that those different identities are sources of strength so long as they are allowed to co-exist and are not competing. When one has got to be superior then weaker ones have to be eliminated or repressed or silenced. If instead you say they all have good things in them then there is a way of all going forward together, in a hackneyed phrase — which however I'm sure we would all support.

Anna Davin has been closely associated with the development of the History Workshop project and has written extensively on gender and social history. This article is a slightly edited version of a talk given by her to the Socialist History Society in November 1997. It is loosely based upon Chapter 12 of her book Growing Up Poor: Home, School and Street in London 1870–1914, *published by Rivers Oram, 1996, which can be consulted for references.*

An Illegal Immigrant in South Africa

Bill McCaig

As part of the 'fringe' activities around the June 1997 conference of the Democratic Left organisation held in Liverpool, the Socialist History Society Joined with Mersey DL to organise a meeting on 'International struggles and the left on Merseyside'. Angela Thew spoke of her time as national secretary of the Chile Solidarity Campaign; Eric Lynch reflected on taking part in a work brigade in Nicaragua in 1989. Terry Egan explained the politics and approaches in forming the ongoing work of the Merseyside Ploughshares Network, which has organised effective protests against arms exports to Indonesia, and solidarity work with the people of East Timor.

The fourth speaker was Bill McCaig, a former merchant seaman who was a member of the Communist Party of Great Britain. In the late sixties he was asked by Gerry Cohen, the Merseyside Party Secretary whether he would take a job which involved sailing to South Africa so as 'to help the ANC and the Party there'. At this time 'probably the main concentration of South African Communist Party members was to be found in London, where they enjoyed good relations with members of the CPGB' (S. Ellis and T. Sechaba, Comrades Against Apartheid: The ANC and the SACP in exile, *James Currey, London, 1992, p.40). There follows an edited transcript of Bill McCaig's talk.*

Clandestine operations

Initially I was involved in propaganda work. There was a need to get material into South Africa, particularly into the hands of dockworkers. I was supplied with propaganda material, which I used to take on the ships. I would go round the holds and distribute it in the cargo, so when the cargo was being taken out, it was there for dockworkers to pick up.

There was also distribution of material within South Africa. You'll understand it was much better for the struggle for material to appear from within South Africa, to be posted within the country, rather than being sent from abroad. So I used to get bundles of mail that I had to take out to South Africa and post ashore. Trying to smuggle bundles of letters out of the docks when you're in a very hot climate presents a bit of a problem as you're wearing few clothes. I'd find myself with bundles of letters strapped round my waist, hoping I wasn't sweating too much! I used to have very loose shirts and put on a few pounds!

I was also asked, whilst we were going up and down the coast, to look over the ports and at possible landing sites on the coast itself for putting guerrillas ashore. Examining the ports was easy but the coast was a different matter. It wasn't a very practical proposition, because I wasn't always on deck and I couldn't really stand there with binoculars, viewing the shoreline. The reason it was difficult to be seen scanning the shoreline was the fact that you didn't know who you were sailing with. For instance, I sailed with an engineer who, while drinking, let slip he was involved with the South African Security Police He had been involved in infiltrating anti-Apartheid groups in the UK and still maintained his contacts.

Secret writing

At the end of 1969–70 they asked me if I could go out to South Africa and I said I would. Initially I went down to London and had discussions with John Gollan, Joe Slovo and Ronnie Kasrils, my contact in London. While there I had some training. I was fixed up with means of communication, pretty primitive but very effective. I was supplied with a book, and an English/Afrikaans dictionary. Certain leaves in the book had been treated with some chemical. I don't know what it was, but it gave a whitish look to the page. What I used to do was to put a piece of paper behind the page, then a piece of glass underneath so I didn't get an imprint in the book and then another page on top of the page and then I'd write my coded message on that. This would leave the underneath sheet with an invisible message on it. I would then destroy the top copy that I had written. In addition to this I used another book for the code. I'd draft out anything I wanted to say. then translate it into a certain code. You had to pick out line numbers, letter numbers You could never make any sense of it unless you had the same codebook. It was very simple, but very effective. They used to communicate with me in that way. I had a supply of capsules you dissolved in boiling water in a tin. This brought out the invisible writing. They also taught me various techniques for seeing if I was being followed. Then I went out to South Africa on a 'holiday'.

It became a couple of year's holiday. I lived in Durban and I got a job on the docks, because I needed to be able to move around the docks to see the opportunities for bringing people in. That was awkward at times. There were sensitive areas in the docks that you weren't allowed in unless you had a pass, e.g. oil depots. I never had a visa to go into South Africa, and officially I was there only for a three-month holiday, so strictly speaking I was an illegal immigrant. So I had a problem getting a valid pass. Fortunately you could borrow somebody else's pass and wend your way round all the dock areas.

Arms shipment

Together with another comrade, I once went down the coast to the Transkei, East London way. I've since found out what the operation was. The ANC had got their hands on a ship they were going to load up with guns and ammunition. It was going to sail down the coast were it would unload the supplies and we going to distribute these around the area. Our job on the shoreside was to go round looking for suitable cache sites, digging big holes, getting pieces of plywood to cover them up and then covering them up again so they couldn't be seen. We took photographs of them so you could actually find them again. It was a bit of a problem finding suitable places You also had the problem of explaining what you were doing if someone saw you digging or just parked in the middle of nowhere. Well, the explanation we came up with involved carrying a toilet roll round with us. So we always came back to the car with this toilet roll, so if anyone was there waiting, it was fairly obvious where we'd been. On top of the car we had fishing rods, so it gave the impression we were going along the coast fishing. That was some of the hardest work I've ever done, digging in rock hard ground to make holes for arms dumps.

As it turned out things had gone wrong on the ship. I found this out later from another Liverpool comrade, Eric Caddick, who'd joined the ship in Somalia. There were obviously some non-comrades in the crew and by the sound of it they'd sabotaged the ship, I believe, they poured sand in the fuel oil and the bearings of the engine had seized up. The Somalis were going to shoot these guys because of what they'd done. They couldn't repair the ship, so the whole thing fell through.

My contacts decided that I should clarify my legal position in South Africa, so I got the correct documents and applied to stay. Anyway I got rejected and consequently I had to pack up the job that I was doing in the docks, move house and disappear.

Cover blown

I got a communication that they were sending some materials to me for another comrade: documents, ID's, money. By this time I was working just outside Durban Airport on an oil refinery and got a message through that somebody wanted to see me at the main gate. As I approached I saw this guy standing there and I thought 'this is a cop'. He started to quiz me, dropping little hints about areas of London (UK) that I knew from my training there. I knew of course this parcel was coming and I presumed they'd got their hands on it. It was obvious he knew something, but I couldn't quite figure out what he did know. He clearly wasn't there to arrest me and the Oil Company wouldn't let him on site and kept him by the gate. For all the power the police had in South Africa he couldn't get inside. This gave me time to collect my thoughts There were police outside the oil refinery in parked cars, obviously keeping tabs on me. When I got home there were police keeping tabs on the flat I was in. So I presumed my position was fairly well blown and I decided to shoot home.

When I got to the airport, the Customs guy said to me. 'You haven't got a valid pass, you're an illegal immigrant. You came for a holiday and you've been here for two years!' I said, 'I've applied to stay, but this is how long it's taken them to refuse me. They've just turned me down. That's why I'm leaving now', 'Okay then,' he said. So off I went.

Back home I rang up Ronnie Kasrils, my contact in London and spoke to him. Of course he's now the Deputy Minister of Defence in South Africa, so his position is slightly changed. It came as a total surprise to him that I was back and that the police in South Africa were involved. What we hadn't known is that the South Africans had already nabbed a comrade and that's how they'd got onto me. The comrade had been receiving money from London and they had got the contact in London to send money to them after his arrest. This is how they had found where the funding was coming from. They looked for other transfers going to people in South Africa from similar sources and came across my name that way. When they contacted me they were only presuming there was some sort of connection between us. So that was how they got onto us, but I didn't know that then. So that was it. End of story.

Delegation to Kurdistan

David Morgan

David Morgan, Secretary of the Socialist History Society and one of our editors, recently took part in a human rights delegation to southern Turkey/Northern Kurdistan to monitor the way the Kurds are treated as they mark their New Year.

We arrived in Diyarbakir, the largest Kurdish city in southern Turkey early Saturday morning in time for Newroz, the Kurdish New Year held on 21 March. Delegations had come from across Europe at the invitation of the Democracy Platform, a loose association of politicians, lawyers, trade unionists and human rights activists. We came to the city named Amed by the Kurds and regarded by them as the capital of Kurdistan to show solidarity and to celebrate with them on the only public occasion on which they are permitted to express their national identity in any meaningful manner. Security was very tight; we were searched as we approached the gathering. The people were wary because of the constant police presence but greeted us with remarkable warmth; it was an emotional experience. I was humbled when one man knelt down and kissed my hand. I did not deserve such treatment. I was not a member of the nobility. The leader of our delegation, Lord Hylton, obviously was and looked the part too and was given an equally warm reception, especially when he joined in the dancing. On a large open field just outside the residential area of Diyarbakir thousands of people had gathered. They were chanting, singing, dancing round the many small fires and just milling around having a good time. There were no overtly political banners; still everyone knew exactly why they were there. Many spoke good English, particularly the students who learn English at school while they are denied the right to study Kurdish. They were anxious for us to spread their message; they wanted our help to gain their freedom from Turkish tyranny. One woman told me how when the army had come to burn down her village they had killed members of her family accusing them of supporting the PKK (Kurdish Workers' Party, Turkey). It was a story that was to become all too familiar; the authorities justified every brutality against the Kurds as combating alleged PKK terrorism. Later we were given evidence of people, including asylum-seekers deported from Germany, being tortured in prison. By accepting Ankara's view that the PKK are simply terrorists the British government unwittingly assists in this repression. A young boy we met, internally displaced to Istanbul, was badly scarred from when three years ago a soldier held him over a fire; his family were PKK suspects and supposedly deserved such treatment. There are in fact about three million displaced villagers from approximately four thousand villages that have been destroyed in this war on the Kurdish people that has gone largely unreported in the Western press for far too long. Many now live in the most appalling conditions in plastic tents and shanty towns outside the city. Tourists to Istanbul never see what is going on.

A helicopter was circling overhead and security officers were perched on the rooftops with cameras. The peaceful, enthusiastic and joyful crowd was later to be attacked by troops ostensibly on the grounds that they were blocking a road; women were beaten in a brutal manner on their breasts and between their legs, according to reports from a German MP who was shocked by what she witnessed. Many arrests were made, including three Italians, one of whom was later sentenced for promoting 'separatism'. The Italian ambassador made fruitless representations and the Italian press gave his incarceration much coverage but he remained in jail. We tried to contact the press in London; they only wanted to know if any 'Brits' had been arrested or injured. Nothing else mattered. Even later, when the police came to our hotel and deported us to Istanbul the press still did not want to know; it is as if there is a conspiracy of silence on the issue.

The Kurds are one of history's most oppressed people and one of the Middle East's oldest cultures. They have no state of their own and are divided by borders drawn up by Britain after the First World War. They survive on the dream of a better future and a passionate determination to preserve their identity in the face of attempts by the Turkish state to deny their very existence. The Kurds of Iraq have endured the gassing of Halabja but even under Saddam Hussein they have greater autonomy than in Turkey where they are simply seen as 'mountain Turks.' It was only a few years ago that illiterate Kurdish villagers faced a fine for every Kurdish word they used when coming to market to sell their produce. Today trade unionists detained by police after a march have their wages docked by their employers; Kurdish children are physically punished at primary school for speaking their mother tongue even though they do not know a word of Turkish. Even private schools are not allowed to teach in Kurdish. Parents fear that the next generation will grow up knowing nothing of their culture and unable to use their own language. Economic necessity may force them to drop Kurdish for Turkish and English.

Since 1995 the Turkish authorities have feebly sought to appropriate the

Newroz festival as their own; they paid a historian to produce a treatise claiming that it was an old Turkish festival. However at official events only a few hundred people turn up and these are mainly students forced to attend; this is in contrast to the tens of thousands joining the unofficial events in the major towns and cities including Istanbul and Ankara where Turkish workers joined with their Kurdish colleagues. It was a privilege to be there celebrating with these courageous people. I shall never forget the warm reception I received. I will be back but I hope one day to celebrate with them in a land that is free.

Reviews

An ambition too far?

John Callaghan (ed.), *Great Power Complex — British Imperialism, International Crises and National Decline* (Pluto Press, London and Chicago, 1997) xiii + 144pp., ISBN 0 7453 1184 9, £9.99 pbk

This latest contribution to the series on 'A Socialist History of Britain' presents a very forceful argument about the extent to which, by the middle of the twentieth century, British imperialism and foreign policy had become drawn into an often uneasy alliance with the needs of the United States of America. Callaghan provides a very detailed and wide-ranging analysis, which offers a long-term evaluation of the driving forces behind British imperialist policy. Considerable attention is devoted to the ways in which the ambitions of successive governments exceeded the short and long-term of both British and Empire economies and the political will to deal positively with the problems thrown up by these world-wide commitments.

The volume is constructed chronologically with an introduction which sets out the wider framework for the rise and decline of the imperial adventure. Each chapter concentrates upon the diplomatic and economic consequences of policy decisions and the growing impact of the internationalisation of capital and capitalism. The reader is made aware of what Callaghan sees as a fateful combination: the increasingly unrealistic desire of governments to preserve Britain's status as a world power, the racism of the 'official mind' which inhibited any significant reviewing of the notion of 'empire' in a more democratic fashion and the international diplomacy which forced Britain and the USA, particularly during and after the Second World War, into an uneasy, but ultimately recognised, dependency on each other.

Above all, this is the first theme which stands out in the analysis, in an often matter-of-fact way, the economic realities of imperial policy, during both wars as well as during the inter-war period, are identified and the long-term difficulties contrasted with the images of empire which were often promoted by industrialists, financiers and politicians alike. Added to this were the economic costs of maintaining a massive naval and military presence across the globe in these years. The British political élite was obsessed with maintaining a notion of superpower status which was unsustainable in the face of changing international relations in the twentieth century and which ran counter to the shifting patterns of capitalist development. Any hint of a move away from such a position was seen as defeatist and likely to produce a self-fulfilling prophecy. Somewhat ironically, the book does provide evidence of the power of positive thinking, in the sense that the strength of desire to retain élite status in world politics did maintain the semblance of British authority in the period concerned although the difficulties being piled up were increasingly destabilising, as the second half of the century has shown.

The inherent racism of the British political élite and the limitations which this imposed upon perceptions of imperial potential are also made explicit. It was not simply that officials denigrated the 'natives' but that their attitudes and policies helped both to create and to underestimate the dynamics of nationalism which developed in many sections of the British Empire during these years. Time and again, Callaghan demonstrates the insensitivity directed towards Africans, Indians and West Indians and reflects that Labour Party ministers and party officials were little better than their Conservative counterparts in this respect. While recognising the 'no doubt sincere desire of reformers like Creech Jones and Rita Hinden' (p.100) for a more positive imperial policy, the political and economic realities of Britain's post-war situation quickly dampened down any vague socialist unease with the principles of imperialism.

Finally, the study emphasises the extent to which American influences were increasingly shaping British foreign policy. The tensions in this relationship are explored in detail and the complexities and dissidences identified. However, by the time of the Cold War, each had come to depend, in admittedly a somewhat uneven relationship, on each other. Strategies in the Middle East, the Mediterranean and in Western Europe in the period after 1945 all need to be seen within this framework.

The arguments are forceful and precise and provide a very clear vision of the decline and fall of British imperial strategies during the twentieth century. In a relatively short volume Callaghan has drawn together a wealth of primary and secondary material and presented the reader with a challenging and very explicit interpretation which will stimulate further debate on this complex issue.

Kenneth Lunn
Portsmouth University

Wool as power
The control of overseas trade in medieval London

Pamela Nightingale, *A Medieval Mercantile Community — The Grocers' Company and the politics and trade of London 1000–1485* (Yale University Press, London, 1995), xi and 640pp., ISBN 0-3000-6325-3, £40.00 hbk

There is an immense amount of detailed research in this book, giving a convincing account of the changing composition and priorities of the élite controlling group among the mercantile community that congregated first among the pepperers, and which subsequently transformed itself into the Grocers' Company, in the late fourteenth century. Dr Nightingale finds the origins of the pepperers' fraternity among the moneyers of the late eleventh and early twelfth centuries, whose profits gave them the capital to extend into the distributive trade in spices. Despite the early formation of a pepperers' fraternity in 1180, the merchants associated with this trade seem to have been relatively insignificant until they broke into the export of wool in the 1290s; (p.93) this is a revision of the classic view of the pepperers' assured dominance of twelfth and thirteenth-century London given by Professor Williams in *Medieval London*. Such dominance however was achieved in the fourteenth century and maintained well into the fifteenth, and sustained by the grocers' key role in the operation of the wool staples through which exports were channelled. However this dominance was increasingly challenged in the fifteenth century by the mercers and drapers, whose exports of cloth boomed as the export trade in raw wool dwindled.

The progress of the pepperers turned grocers is described in narrative format, with at times a year-by-year account of the activities of the leading merchants. This does create considerable problems of coherence. I would strongly recommend anyone unfamiliar with medieval urban history to read the conclusion first in order to appreciate the shape of the argument, otherwise there is the danger of being lost in a welter of detail. Some of this detail is not justified; for example the account of the coinage of Muslim Spain (p.38) is more appropriate to a specialist article. Other detail is introduced in a rather indiscriminate manner: a discussion of recruitment into the pepperers' trade and the transfer of this trade from alien to indigenous merchants is broken by a paragraph on the sanitary problems of medieval London; (p.102) the analysis of the changing nature of the Grocers' Company on page 222 is interrupted by a topographical description of Bucklersbury. In a book of this length such digressions do tax the reader.

There is a theoretical framework underlying this narrative. The author is a monetarist and does make a strong case for the significance of the flow of bullion for short-term fluctuations in the economy. But the narrative structure militates against any clear demonstration of the long-term significance of the coinage as against other factors influencing the economy and trade, and the matter is not dealt with at any point in a theoretical way. Whilst Dr Nightingale is secure and impressive operating within her own methodology, she can be rather dismissive of any alternative interpretations of the evidence and this is particularly dangerous given the limited scope of the book, which is about the trading operations of a small group of the élite written from the records of the élite. Dr Nightingale has no time for the idea of class conflict and shares the views of those historians who see the urban community as a relatively harmonious whole, marked by consensus. No substantial evidence is offered for this optimistic assessment however, and no systematic investigation made of any group of people other than the leading exporters. On page 565 the claim is made that 'the humblest apprentice...had every hope of rising in his company, but this uncritical restatement of the theory of removable inequalities is as far as the discussion of class relations goes. Elsewhere when the issue is raised and could be further investigated it is simply sidestepped. (pp.187, 224, 290, 311)

The neglect is the more serious because Dr Nightingale's discussion of the upheavals in London in the reign of Richard II are largely designed to refute an interpretation of events that lays emphasis on class conflict. The rivalry of the grocer's leader, Nicholas Brembre and John of Northampton, the leader of the drapers has been seen in a variety of ways: conflict between victuallers and manufacturers, between capitalists and artisans, or as rivalry within the merchant class. Dr Nightingale opts for the last of these interpretations and produces ample evidence to show how such rivalries operated. But the wider context of relationships between merchants and manufactures is lacking, leaving many questions about why John of Northampton attracted his support from the manufacturing crafts unanswered. In particular Northampton relied on the tailors and irrespective of his motives, the relationships between grocers and tailors need more clarification, for in the absence of an effective fraternity of their own in the late fourteenth century (see below) many grocers joined the Tailors' Fraternity of St John the Baptist. (p.294) It has also to be said that Dr Nightingale's account of this conflict is violently partisan. Northampton's associates are called 'henchmen' and 'the mafia'; those of Brembre are 'allies'. However there is no reason to suppose that the sectional interests of Northampton were unusual or indeed exceptionally despicable. Dr Nightingale writes of the grocers themselves that 'the structure of the Company made it possible for a few powerful men to control its policy, which explains why the interests of the staplers dominated it for so long, even when they were only a small group within the Company'. (p.250) This small, powerful élite wanted to extend its domination to the government of London by controlling the aldermannic bench as far as possible in the late fourteenth and early fifteenth centuries. The leading grocers had for a long time minimal interest in the spiritual and commensual aspects of their own Company; they were indifferent to fostering a sense of communality with the majority of their fellow master grocers (until their dominance of the admermannic bench was threatened in the latter part of the fifteenth century and they needed to find a new power base). In the late fourteenth century, according to Dr Nightingale, so many of the élite grocers 'served as aldermen that the Guildhall made up for the lack of a Grocers' Hall, and their civic duties left them no time for the kind of fraternising congenial to the retailers'. It seems then wilfully perverse to state that men as determinedly power hungry and exclusive as this were restricting the position of alderman in the late fifteenth century to those worthy of at least £1000 in order 'to protect the least well off'. (p.567)

The problems with this book arise because it is addressed to two different audiences. It is on the one hand a 'Hooray for the Grocers' and on the other a scholarly study of certain aspects of the medieval mercantile community. Inevitably it falls between two stools, which is a great pity because there is so much detailed and challenging information in it, but it is information which could have been better presented in a more analytical and succinct format.

Dr Heather Swanton
University of Birmingham

Of Icons and Men

John Lee Anderson. *Che Guevara: A revolutionary life* (Bantam Press, London, 1997) xv and 814pp., ISBN 0-5930-3403-1, £25.00 hbk

The most heated arguments of my youth were about Ernesto 'Che' Guevara. They were tangled and ambivalent: Che the icon kept getting mixed up with Guevara the political figure. In the Italy of the late 1960s, at the height of the students' movement, it was the icon that we knew best. Like most of my generation I could not escape its power but felt uneasy about what it represented. Guevara's politics did not convince me. Thirty years of political experience later I am sure my misgivings were correct. Anderson's massive, detailed biography provides further evidence for them, even though reading this book is like plunging back into old arguments with the comrades of my youth.

The icon we needed

An icon, by definition, is someone who looks like what they represent, and Che undoubtedly looked the part. He was 'the revolution made flesh', as Richard Gott aptly describes him. In the 1960s, his image was everywhere, promoted by an Italian left-wing publisher, Feltrinelli, whose marketing instincts were probably more acute than his political analysis. What we knew then of Guevara's politics was superficial and bitty. We approved of his having read Freud and Jung as well as Marx and Mao. We read some of his speeches and writing on guerrilla warfare but, mainly, we read between the lines of what he said and did, drawing the conclusions we needed.

We wanted a revolutionary who had embraced armed struggle, a link forward to change and back to our own history of armed liberation — the partisans' resistance against Fascism and Nazi invasion, whose stories and myths we had grown up with. We needed someone who was tied to the communist parties that defined our own political space but was critical of their bureaucracies and compromises. Someone prepared to live out his principles, socially unconventional and not motivated by material privileges and comforts.

Most of all we needed a promise that the class gap between us, privileged students, and the poor in our own country and in the rest of the world could be bridged. Che, as Jorge Castaneda has pointed out in his influential book on the Latin American Left, was 'the symbol of an intellectual middle class horrified by the intolerable distance between itself and the rest of society, by the abyss that separated it from the vast and undifferentiated universe of the poor.'

For those of us who did not come from the middle class 'the intolerable distance' was inside ourselves and within our own families. To survive economically, my parents had left the countryside and lived in a class limbo, cut off from the conditions that had made them but not yet part of anything else. I had been shaped by the customs, beliefs and storytelling of a peasantry that was disappearing, whose material world I did not share. Che's call for 'revolution in the countryside' appealed to a nostalgia of the self and invited my scepticism — I knew the difficulties of bridging class abysses. My middle-class comrades were more enthusiastic, oblivious to our own history of disastrous attempts at liberating the peasantry from outside.

What if some of that need is still around? Icons can be recycled as long as they are energetically marketed and the social conditions are right. Could Che become an icon again now that the distance between rich and poor keeps widening, there is suspicion of party politics among young people, and individual integrity and lifestyle are seen as one of the few touchstones? With a spate of new books, documentaries and a film in the making, it would not be surprising to see Che's image on mugs, chests and walls once again.

Becoming Che

Ernesto Guevara's life thoroughly qualified him for his role as an icon. The son of an impoverished Argentinian aristocratic family, he grew up in the midst of contradictions and dislocations: privilege and money worries; the social rituals and prejudices of his class together with unconventional behaviour and liberal political attitudes; patriarchal structures inhabited by ineffectual, charming men and strong, intellectual women; freedom bordering on emotional neglect and intense concern, especially for his health (he suffered from severe asthma from early childhood). By his early twenties, he was already many of the things that would fit him for his role as a cultural and ethical icon: 'an attractive oddball', 'eccentric in appearance', someone who 'defied definition' and had a daredevil physical courage. He read widely and was close to politically active people but was not involved in Argentinian politics. 'More than a political person' he was 'someone with an ethical posture'.

From Argentinian politics and Peron's success, he drew the lesson that 'strong leadership and a willingness to use force to meet one's goals' were crucial. But his political education really began when he started travelling around South and Central America. Only when outside his own country and social context did he become aware of the appalling conditions in which the majority of people lived.

His education, however, was rather skewed. His medical training and attitudes often took him to places where misery, exclusion and marginalisation were most evident — leper colonies, hospitals, prisons, and police stations. Or he would be the guest of family friends and contacts — comfortable middle-class professionals and intellectuals.

He made contact with workers and peasants but he did not really have much experience or understanding of the organised working class and other forms of mass organisation. Travelling from place to place he was inevitably inclined towards broad-brush generalisations rather than careful analysis of the specific circumstances of each country. His political reactions were a kind of panAmerican nationalism with a tendency to reduce all the problems of the continent to US imperialism.

Unbecoming politics

Guevara, like many others, had to step outside his own social context and country to become fully aware of injustice and exploitation. But he could not step back and turn this general awareness into more concrete and detailed forms of analysis and political practice. For most of his formative years, he remained a political outsider, a witness to a continent that was changing at incredible speed. He could grasp it only in generalities. In this sense Che is a fitting icon for a certain kind of 'internationalism' that cannot make the lessons it learns elsewhere relevant to its own context and articulates itself around the common denominator of a 'single enemy' — once US imperialism, now globalisation. 'In the name of international proletarianism we commit errors that can be very costly,' Guevara admitted in a letter to Fidel Castro many years later, at the end of his disastrous expedition to the Congo.

Che's first political involvement was with the Guatemalan revolution in 1954 when the reforming government of Arbenz was in power. His role, like the government, was short-lived as a CIA-backed coup ousted Arbenz later that year. The experience had a profound effect on Guevara, who drew one main lesson from it: power had to be defended with force. There are undoubtedly times when 'the people in arms' have to defend themselves and their structures of power, but Guevara and many of his contemporaries tended to overemphasise the arms rather than the people. His subsequent involvement with the Cuban guerrilla army and the victory of Castro's July 26 Movement reinforced his military view of revolution and led him to develop the notion of the 'foco' — a small guerrilla group, usually based in the countryside, that would spark off insurrection through military confrontation. For Guevara, armed struggle became not only a necessary but a sufficient condition for revolution — a conclusion that was to have disastrous effects for him and many others.

The Cuban conflict was relatively short in comparison with the major guerrilla wars that were to follow in Columbia, Nicaragua, Guatemala, and El Salvador. It was more of a military operation than a popular war; indeed, military issues figure more prominently in Anderson's account of Guevara's two years in the Sierra Maestra than issues of popular mobilisation, education or governance. Guevara's role in the war was mainly military and organisational. He was clearly an intrepid soldier, a skilled and charismatic military leader and a good organiser but it's doubtful that, before or after the Cuban revolution, he understood the importance of constructing and maintaining political alliances and building mass organisations. As Richard Gott has said, 'his skills as a political operative can now clearly be seen to have been less than adequate.' Ironically for someone who is so often invoked as a symbol of revolution, he had a reductive and vanguardist view of revolutionary conflict.

Anderson tells us that 'in the battlegrounds of Burma, El Salvador, Western Sahara, and even in Muslim Afghanistan, I found that Che remained a figure of veneration for guerrillas of all kinds. 'Veneration', perhaps — real guerrillas need their icons and symbols too. Less than ten years after Guevara's death, however, a second wave of Latin American guerrillas, especially in Central America, was fighting quite a different kind of war. 'We have understood that it is people that have to wage war,' declared Salvador Caetano Carpio, one of the founders of the Salvadorean FMLN, 'and armed groups should not turn themselves into a handful of heroes who have no links with the masses and will spare them the problem of carrying out a revolution.'

Guevara made too much of war. Wars have powerful effects on both those who participate and on the society as a whole but they are not in themselves revolutions. They draw people together in temporary convergence of interests, an intensity of life-and-death sharing, but they are not, as Guevara thought, 'the ideal circumstance in which to achieve a socialist consciousness.'

Armed struggle is sometimes a necessity but not a guarantee of radicalism. Guevara often judged his men — he did not allow women combatants — by whether or not 'they passed the test' of combat. It is seems at times that Anderson applies a similar measure to Guevara's politics. But should we not judge political movements by the effects they have rather than by how hard they fight?

Anderson makes it clear that the political was also personal for Guevara: 'It is hard to escape the sense that Che's deeply felt desire....to become part of a group derived from the inherent isolation imposed by his asthma....in this communal life of guerrilla war, none suffered alone; the interdependency wrought by the need to survive was mutual....Quite possibly it was this sense of sharing, more than any other factors, that gave rise to his intense personal reverence for the ethos of guerrilla life.' 'He needed the sierra,' was Eduardo Galeano's verdict after meeting Guevara in 1964 just before he embarked on the last two expeditions of his life. At last, an admission that there might have been, as there usually is, a relationship between who Guevara was as a person and his political choices and positions.

Yet, Anderson still falls into the gushing sentimentality of Guevara's own prose where revolutionaries are described as 'self-sacrificing' heroes, 'violent, seductive, and cold killing machines' who 'cannot descend, with small doses of daily affection, to the places where ordinary men put their love into practice.' Che, Anderson tells us, is 'the ultimate revolutionary icon, his eyes seeming to stare boldly into the future, his very face symbolising a virile embodiment of outrage at social injustice.' 'New men' or old arguments?

Maria Black

Maria Black is an Italian psycholinguist. She has been involved with popular movements in Central America and with the FMLN in El Salvador

Is the Eastern European transformation unique?

Geoffrey Pridham and Tatu Vanhanen (eds), *Democratisation in Eastern Europe* (Routledge, London, 1994) xiv and 274pp., £12.99 pbk, ISBN 0-415-11064-5

R.J. Crampton, *Eastern Europe in the Twentieth Century* (Routledge, London, 1994) xx and 475pp., £14.99 pbk, ISBN 0-415-05346-3

How should we interpret the massive changes that have taken place in Eastern Europe over the past six years? Are they primarily concerned with the creation of the institutions of political democracy, or should that be seen as but one element in a more global transformation? Is this a completely new and unique process or is it essentially a repeat of transformations that have taken place elsewhere? Does the Communist past still play a role in shaping events or have the countries of Eastern Europe now returned to some 'natural' form of which they were for forty years robbed by an alien, but mercifully transient, system?

The collection edited by Pridham and Vanhanen, based on a workshop held in March 1991, makes a valuable, if incomplete, contribution to answering these and other questions. Its starting point is a quest for a possible explanation for the transformation of the political systems across the region, seeking explanations for both why the Communist system collapsed and for why democratisation is taking its particular and varied forms. The authors seek analogies with previous democratic transformations, begin to search for differences between Eastern European countries themselves and ask how complete the break has been from the recent Communist, and more distant pre-Communist, pasts.

Geoffrey Pridham has built his recent reputation on studies of democratisation in Southern Europe in the 1970s and tries to apply very much the same methodology here. Democratisation itself is seen as the creation of institutional structures, including above all political parties. It involves a 'liberalisation', followed by a 'consolidation', phase. To explain the transformation, he looks at 'functionalist' and 'genetic' approaches. The former seek causes in social structures that may develop and change over long periods of time. The latter concentrate on recent events involving political choices. Other contributors take this approach further, including one which uses statistical tests with a string of variables to represent the level of social development — such as literacy, levels of education, and extent of individual ownership — to predict which of the world's countries could be expected to develop a stable political democracy. The conclusion there is that the transformations in some parts of Eastern Europe were long overdue.

The trouble with this approach is its narrow restriction within the framework of political science. This is inadequate for two reasons. The first is that it omits reference to the uniqueness of the Communist period. The political transformations in Eastern Europe do have some analogies with those in Latin America, Southern Europe in the 1970s and Western Europe after 1945. Essentially, however, they cannot be divorced from the system that preceded them. The second reason is that the transformations that have taken place have not focused on the political system alone. Their causes, and their course, have been crucially influenced by, and intertwined with, other economic and social changes. In this they clearly do differ from democratisations in Southern Europe.

Much of this is taken up by other contributors. As soon as the question is broached of the kind of parties to be expected, the influence of other factors becomes clear. The most important alternative perspective is provided by Michael Waller who starts by emphasising that the democratic transformation involves more than just the creation of political parties. Moreover, the process need not be leading to political structures familiar in parts of Western Europe. The future to him remains rather opaque. Indeed, his interpretation eschews cosy analogies by placing far more emphasis on historical factors that may be specific to each country. In particular, he insists that the Communist period itself has left a strong imprint which is a distinguishing, and to some extent a uniting, feature of the Eastern European transformations. He even tries to find hints for the development of post-1989 politics in the movements that emerged before that date. He probably overstates this. Much of the thinking of that period now seems to have been swept aside amid the immense social changes — again confirming the inadequacy of a narrow focus on political structures alone.

Nevertheless, this and several other contributions to the collection do point to the need for a greater awareness of the histories of the individual countries. Unfortunately, the book by Crampton is rather disappointing and does not help much for answering the questions posed by recent events. It covers the period from 1918 to 1991 in the former Communist countries of Eastern Europe, including the GDR and the Baltic countries from the former Soviet Union. It is not a work that seeks to pose, let alone answer, broad questions. Thus we do not learn whether the area is brought together by anything more than geography or the accident of a recent political experience. The questions of what might differentiate the countries of the region is never addressed in any systematic way.

It is, then, not much help in identifying direct influences from the past. This is unfortunate when recent developments do at least seem to echo what went before. Thus the position, attitudes and behaviour of Poland's President Walesa are often likened to those of Pilsudski from the inter-war period. The apparent stability of inter-war Czechoslovak democracy is sometimes quoted as a possible explanation for the recent consolidation of Czech political life. On closer inspection, these similarities may be more imagined than real. In both cases the issues shaping political life differ markedly from those of the interwar period. Nevertheless, without more of an attempt to explain what happened in earlier periods it is impossible to know whether apparent similarities reflect coincidence, the impact of lasting factors — such as geographical location — or the impact of an awareness of past history itself.

Indeed, Crampton's work is rather an old-fashioned approach to history. There is nothing systematic on social or economic changes. The deeper reasons for the failure of the Communist systems are never really explored.

One table, the only one in the book, purports to indicate the slow growth in living standards, but a rider explains that the figures are not reliable, giving too favourable an impression of Eastern Europe's performance.

The greatest criticism, however, is that the book is a disaster as a factual account. Events that might be considered important, such as the creation of the Berlin Wall, are referred to as if we knew all about them already. Others of lesser importance, such as the decision by the Slovak writer Ladislav Mnacko to live in Israel in 1967, are given substantial prominence. Far too many issues of fact that are still up for debate are treated as if settled, with little referencing of sources. Indeed, there seem to be no open questions in this account. There are also simply too many identifiable factual errors and distortions — often running to several on the same page. These frequently relate to important issues that could be crucial to an interpretation of events. Indeed, the best part of the book is probably the bibliography. Unfortunately, the author has not made effective use of the sources he lists.

Martin Myant
Martin Myant teaches at Paisley University
and has written extensively on Eastern Europe

Young Germans against the Nazis

Alfred Fleischacker (ed.), *Das War Unser Leben: Erinnerungen und dockumente zur der Freien Deutschen Jügend in Grossbritannien 1939–1946*, Feus Leben, Berlin, 1996

The history of German youth organisations in Britain during the Second World War has left little trace, except in the memory of a decreasing number of survivors. It was not until 1991 that two former members of the Free German Youth in Great Britain sent out a letter inviting contributions to a projected book. The editor of the resulting collection of reminiscences and documents sounds somewhat apologetic when he writes in the introduction that much of what has been contributed seems 'undramatic, even banal'. But, he adds, 'historians should rejoice with me that at least a good dozen of us have recorded what would otherwise be irretrievable'.

The book makes no pretensions to offering more than material drawn from the memories of an *ad hoc* group of people after a fifty-year interval, although a brief factual history of the organisation is included as well as some of its programmatic statements and other documents. Nevertheless, the project has been very worth while, not only by filling a gap in German history, but also for historians of British youth organisations.

The reason for the long silence on this subject is a sad reflection of postwar developments. When the Free German Youth was established in 1946 in the then Soviet Occupation Zone, members of the FGY GB were amongst the leading activists who went 'back home'. Yet their British connection was soon frowned upon in the German Democratic Republic. It is alleged that Party leader Honecker himself saw to it that a veil was drawn over their undesirable past....Cold War Stalinism meant that anybody with roots in, or connections, to the West was to be regarded as suspicious. And, no doubt, the fact that a majority of the young former refugees were Jewish, often from bourgeois backgrounds, also played a part in how they were seen by communist officialdom in the GDR. As for West Germany, it seems that there was never any interest in an anti-fascist organisation 'tainted' with communist connections.

The constitution of the FGY GB, from July 1939, states that it 'is an independent organisation and is linked to no party. It works closely with all forces which stand for uniting all German friends of freedom and peace', in fact, its formation and aims were fully in line with the People's Front policy of the Comintern. The Communist Party of Germany in exile exercised a paternal influence. On the British side, broad front organisations such as the British Youth Assembly, and later the International Youth Council, gave all the help and support they could to the refugee youth. In view of the nature of this publication the wider picture is largely lacking...relations with British youth groups up and down the country, and with refugee groups of other nationalities, including the Czechs, Austrians, and Spanish, would no doubt be worth looking into.

In the early days, the bulk of the FGY GB membership must have been unpolitical. They arrived in the 'children's transports', following the Kristallnacht pogrom of November 1938. Aged between 14 and 18, they came without their parents, whom most were never to see again. The FGY offered practical support and friendship. Political awareness was stimulated unwittingly by the British government through the internment of 'enemy aliens'. This shameful episode has been fairly well documented, but here we have some recorded experiences of those who were boys at the time. They remember a time of political awakening and education, guided by socialist and, especially, communist internees. The camps thus became hotbeds of 'subversive' thinking which later led to much dedicated and effective work for the war effort. In due course, some of the young Germans were allowed to join the British armed forces, and in April 1946 there were still 96 FGY members serving.

What shines through these documents and the memories of these fighters against Nazism is the idealism of young Germans encouraged by their organisation to prepare for rebuilding their country as a free, democratic and — they hoped — socialist state. Most of the FGY members who returned home settled in the east. 'In those days,' writes Alfred Fleischacker, 'we dreamed not only of a better world after the defeat of the brown barbarism, but also that we would be able to take part in shaping a new epoch. The century now passing has taught us that many of us were too credulous.'

Marian Fagan

Marian Fagan is a member of the Socialist History Society

British and US labour movements

Neville Kirk, *Labour and Society in Britain and the USA,* Vol.1, *Capitalism, Custom, and Protest, 1780–1850* (Scolar Press, London, 1994) ISBN 1-85928-021-8, 226pp.; Vol.2, *Challenge and Accomodation, 1850–1939* (Scolar Press, London, 1994) ISBN 1-95928-022-6, 424pp., £49.50 hbk

Labour history, in most countries and certainly our own, is still mostly taught and analysed within the boundaries of particular societies. Agreed that there has been improvement in recent years, and it is one of the many merits of these two volumes by Neville Kirk that we are presented with a wide-ranging comparative study of British and American labour movements over the whole period of their history until the Second World War. The amplitude and extent of sources quoted is impressive throughout.

Historians of American labour have for many years argued for the qualitative differences between the evolution of political ideas and their corresponding organisation in the United States compared with their opposite groups in Britain and western Europe. This theory of 'exceptionalism' has been increasingly criticised in the past decade or so by American historians. The writings of Sean Wilentz and others have demonstrated in vigorous terms that the traditional thesis of the American metropolitan working class with quite different patterns of thought and behaviour from their counterparts across the Atlantic must now be considered untenable. Neville Kirk accepts this position and his own discussion of 'exceptionalism' offers a very helpful guide to the arguments and the evidence. It is, of course, a complex matter, for while it is recognised that American workers turned, in varying ways, to politics independent of the existing order, it is also the frequency of their failures which must be explained. Beginning in the later eighteenth century popular protest movements in America and Britain reached their maturity in the 1830s and 1840s; and in both there were significant breaks in the traditions which were developing, during the decade of the 1940s. In America the widespread economic depression between 1837 and 1842 seriously undermined the progress in radical ideas and organisations that already existed, while in Britain the three successive confrontations of Chartism with the bourgeois State 1839–40, 1842 and 1843 ended with the disintegration of the national movement that had been represented by Feargus O'Connor and the *Northern Star*. Then followed a political consciousness that, with exceptions, adopted a more limited, reformist approach until the emergence once again of a socialist movement and socialist ideas. In America the Civil War, immigration on a now massive scale, the very rapid growth of manufacturing and its associated labour force provided both similarities and quite marked differences with the working-class movement in Britain.

The author's central theoretical concern is with the 'issues of class making and class breaking' and he naturally pays close attention to the dynamic changes constantly introduced by the deepening and broadening consequences of the onward march of capitalism. What we have is the continuous replacement of old by new technologies and the introduction of new forms of entreprenueial practice and operation. It is, as we know, the maximisation of profit that has been the driving force of change, and Kirk analyses what was happening in the second quarter of the nineteenth century, in both Britain and America, with words that could apply, using the cliché *mutatis mutandis*, to Thatcher's Britain in the 1980s: 'sub-contracting, putting-out, beating down wages, increasing hours of work, undermining apprenticeship and employing cheap labour'.

The sense of class, and the acceptance of trade unionism as an essential corrective to the power of employers, were more marked in Britain than in the United States. We have the paradox in the latter country that while strikes were often much more violently conducted, by employers as well as the coercive powers of State and Federal governments, than would have been acceptable in the United Kingdom, the patterns of voting were often in conservative terms. This is not to suggest that strikes and lock-outs in Britain were conducted in gentlemanly ways, nor is it to infer that industrial action was indissolubly linked with an increased political radicalism on the part of the workers involved. Kirk very properly notes that the political affiliations which working men had with liberalism and the Liberal Party — and with conservatism and the Conservative Party — were dissolved more slowly than has often been appreciated, but the secular trend towards independent working-class politics up to the end of this period was a good deal more pronounced than in America; and he gives full weight to the factors of racism and ethnicity as obfuscating the sense of class.

The concluding hundred pages of volume 2 are concerned with the industrial relations and labour politics of the two countries during the interwar years and the author suggests that the contrasts of this period require a more specifically nationally based analysis. The most obvious difference is the emergence of the Labour Party in Britain as the main opposition party to the Conservatives, while in the US the fierce industrial struggles of the 1930s were subordinated and contained within a trade union objective. By the end of the decade the Democratic Party was still a coalition of big capitalists, southern planters and a much larger weighting of industrial workers than ever before. Kirk has some sober comments on the cautious politics of the Labour and Trade Union leaderships in Britain during this decade.

In a large-scale study of over 600 pages there are inevitably matters on which there will be disagreement. I will mention one which I regard as having been much neglected by socialist historians in recent years — as compared with the 1970s and early 1980s — and which ought to return as a major concern. It is the question of British economic decline in the twentieth century. In my view the entrepreneurial failure on the part of British management was already a fact of economic life in the closing decades of the nineteenth century. I adduce only two of a complex of factors and I am not unaware of many others. The first relates to the particular way in which technological change came about during the early decades of industrialisation in Britain: a matter mostly of empirical experimentation remote from the science laboratory. As a Frenchman said after visiting the iron works of North Staffordshire at the end of the 1860s: '*Rien ne vaut que le practical man*': an attitude which helps to explain the very low totals of engineers and scientifically trained technicians on the eve of the First World War. And the second reason which greatly assisted the complacency of the British managerial classes was the opportunity to continue to export our traditional manufactures to both the Empire and other countries in the first stage of their industrial development at a time when electricity and steel were beginning to revolutionise technical innovation. By 1914 productivity levels in Britain were already below those in the United States and Germany, and the structure of our foreign trade was already failing to match the growth areas in world trade.

This is not the way to bring a review of Neville Kirk's important work to a proper conclusions. He has given us an impressively documented analysis, lucidly written, that both the university teacher and her/his students will find rewarding. Those who believe in the importance and intellectual usefulness of comparative history, as indeed we all should, are much in his debt, not least for the bibliographic introduction to his own reading.

John Saville
John Saville is emeritus professor at Hull University and a notable contributor to labour movement historiography

Thrusting women into the socialist agenda

Clarissa Campbell Orr (ed.), *Wollstonecraft's Daughters: Womanhood in England and France, 1780–1920* (Manchester University Press, 1996), 206pp., ISBN 0-7190 4241-0, £40.00 hbk

This book is well produced, illustrated, with references conveniently placed at the end of each chapter. Although individual chapters are, regrettably, too short to allow arguments to be fully developed, the comparative approach of the book as a whole is useful. For example, Clarissa Campbell Orr's first chapter will be of value to students of history, women's history and women's studies. She writes of the ambivalent message, derived partly from the secretive model of the *Ancien Regime*, that the 'masculinist, even misogynist' Jacobin culture sent to women and subsequently contrasts this to the different model of republican politics in Geneva, where there was space for women such as Albertine Necker de Saussure to be active 'socially, culturally and to some extent intellectually' (p.65). On a more basic level, how much more attractive a *Maison de Refuge* sounds than a workhouse.

'Thrusting them into the socialist agenda' is Maire Fedelma Cross's description of Flora Tristan's championship of women's rights in nineteenth century France. Cross outlines Tristan's importance in the reclamation of Mary Wollstonecraft's reputation; indeed, Flora Tristan has more claim than some of the subjects of this book to Wollstonecraft's inheritance, as she was both politically intelligent and similarly concerned with issues of oppression and equal rights across gender boundaries and for workers. This collection of conference papers includes those on other women, such as Sarah Stickney Ellis and Elizabeth Hamilton, whose connection to the witness to the French revolution and colleague of Tom Paine is harder to trace. However, the political left is informed by many strands; Wollstonecraft and Paine, of course, were Girondins rather than the Jacobins they were labelled; and a prescriptive approach begs the question of the relationship of gender and class. A convincing case is indicated in several papers that capitalism and patriarchy are twin products of industrialisation, neither of which can be successfully challenged in isolation. It is no coincidence that the backlash against feminism, from Mary Wollstonecraft's time to our own, happens at times of political oppression.

Class and gender

Middle-class men do not have to apologise for identification with working-class activity (Proudhon, Marx, Engels) and it is accepted that to include aristocratic men in historical enquiry will enlighten our understanding of the operation of power. K.D. Reynolds usefully illustrates that aristocratic women's activity, directed to the accretion of power and inspired by ideals of élite social reproduction and closure, ignored by historians of class, has also been dismissed by historians of gender, so that we fail to address one of the ways in which capitalism and patriarchy are sustained: 'aristocratic women are difficult to fit into the discourses of oppression and liberation which still dominate...British women's history'. (p.94) One might except the 'Ladies' of Langham Place and the *English Women's Journal*, whose championship of women's right to work is referred to in several chapters. The muddled thinking which led one of their contacts, Maria Rye, to conduct to the colonies Lancashire mill women and children from London workhouses and streets, is an appalling example of the worst type of middle-class philanthropy. Many feminists across both sides of the Channel did attempt, with greater sensitivity, to organise women across class boundaries. Flora Tristan is the best example. Cross shows that both Wollstonecraft and Tristan learnt about the realities of class from their invidious positions as ladies' companions. The waste of talent they observed caused both to insist on all women's rights to education. Tristan tried to ally women and workers in her idealistic *Union Ouvriere*; that she failed does not diminish the importance of her attempt. The lesson Tristan drew was that 'the working class must liberate itself'; (p.129) she was one of the first to articulate this politics, that each person/group of people has to struggle for their own rights; that empowerment is not in the gift of the philanthropist. We have still to discover a successful way of aggregating such discoveries into one programme.

Gender and ethnicity

Jane Rendall writes that Elizabeth Hamilton, concerned with the 'ways in which British women could participate in shaping the national character' when recording the life of Agrippina, perceived history as a flawed record: 'devoted mainly to men as "the conquerors and disturbers of the earth"'.

(p.82) Rendall discusses the process by which gender stereotypes and the idea of nationhood developed by impacting on each other, illuminating the nexus between the social construction of both gender and ethnicity. In this context, Felicia Gordon's discussion of Edith Simcox's work is informative. Writing 'the history of peace', studying ancient civilisations where domestic, 'maternal' culture was the antithesis of capitalist patriarchy and women's contribution was valued, Simcox failed to deal with slavery: 'the issue of racial hierarchy...remains a stumbling block — to Simcox's socialist and feminist vision'. (p.181) Gordon's paper imaginatively deconstructs her subject's politics, here offering us the insight that socialism 'might be the nineteenth century experience of a maternal or domestic culture'.

Wollstonecraft's legacy

For the rest, this collection deals with two other main subjects one, the contrast between the British Dissenting and French Roman Catholic traditions, with examples of how the latter has empowered women by providing them with a public place and voice and two, women's search for fulfilling and gainful employment and the right to engage in scholarly activity. Clarissa Campbell Orr, in her introductory chapter, identifies three main themes, religion and the empowerment of women, women's engagement in the human sciences and the impact of the French revolution on motherhood and conduct literature. In such a diverse collection, each reader will identify their own areas of interest. Felicia Gordon asks whether we can speak of a tradition in feminist thought and this book shows us the diversity of feminists — reactionary (Maria Rye), socialist (Tristan, Simcox, Pelletier). Cross reminds us that labels such as 'socialist' or 'liberal' feminist are not helpful, a point with which many women's studies teachers will agree. Addressing a Western, male tradition of scholarship, feminists are unlikely to be able to trace an untrammelled line of progression, from Wollstonecraft through her legatees, as each had to operate in a more or less hostile world and varying strategies of survival developed. Nevertheless, Orr makes a central point, entirely relevant to those seeking to promote equal rights today: 'The legacy of the revolution remained a permanent contrast in the modern political culture of the two countries; latterly, women's rights have been better protected by European Union directives, based on a continental model of citizenship, than they have been under Britain's parliamentary tradition'. (p.5) *Vivat Regina?*

Christine Collette
Christine Collette teaches at Edge Hill University College

The dockers' dilemma

Jim Phillips, *The Great Alliance — Economic recovery and the problems of power, 1945–1951* (Pluto Press, 1996), 157pp., ISBN 0-7453-1038-9, £40.00 hbk, ISBN 0-7453-1037-0, £12.99 pbk

The 1945–51 Labour government has been very much on everyone's mind. In 1995, New Labour remembered the 1945 General Election victory, and Tony Blair gave a valedictory lecture praising the first majority Labour government — whilst carefully drawing a firm line underneath their achievements. Blair told his audience that the next Labour government would honour the spirit of the 1945 men and women, but would not replicate their perspective or re-enact their statutes. Times had changed.

Jim Phillips's book, *The Great Alliance*, is written from this standpoint. He is interested in the 1945–51 Labour government not merely as a historian, but also because '...in the 1990s the experiences of the Attlee and Wilson governments stand as valuable lessons for "New Labour"....Attlee and other Labour leaders in the middle of the century unambiguously accepted trade unions for what they were and remain, popular and democratic institutions representing millions of working people. Only through sharing the Attlee government's appraisal of the positive value of trade unionism, and by seeking to engage the active and voluntary co-operation of the trade union movement, can a future Labour government hope to survive and flourish.' (Final paragraph of *The Great Alliance*, p.136.) Scholars of the postwar period, as well as those New Labour members and current trade unionists will find Phillips's book a fascinating read. He writes fluently and provides food for thought and sober reflection.

The arresting picture on the cover of the paperback edition, 'stevedores handling bagged sugar, 1940', is actually much more revealing of its contents than the actual title. Apart from the introductory and concluding chapters, *The Great Alliance* concentrates on the docks. There is a detailed account of the political undercurrents, cross-currents inside the TGWU, and class conflicts involved in three major unofficial dock strikes which occurred during the 1945–51 Labour government's tenure, the October 1945 Dockers Charter strike, the 'zinc oxide' strike of June 1948 and the series of strikes in May–July 1949 which originated in dockers' refusal to handle cargo from Canadian ships during a dispute of the Canadian Seamen's Union.

According to the preface, these strikes were chosen because: 'it was in the docks that the Labour Alliance [between the Labour Party and the

TUC] was at its most important, but for historical reasons, it was also at its most vulnerable.' (p.vii) However, the text does not make the case for their special significance. The reader can see that they were important in the Government's fortunes, and certainly influenced the relationship between the Transport and General Workers' Union and its members in the docks. It is a revealing snapshot of one part of the wider picture. But there is no evidence offered about the many other sources of industrial conflict with which the Labour government wrestled, e.g. in the newly nationalised industries or engineering.

Phillips treats the difficult issues underlying the unofficial dock strikes with clarity. Such admirable succinctness leads the reader to see clearly those background areas in the wider picture which are still unresolved by labour historians.

The Cold War and the British trade union movement

Phillips repeats the received wisdom that the British trade-union movement was significantly split by anti-communist offensives. In support, he cites the TUC General Council's anti-communist statements of 1948 and 1949 and the TGWU's ban on Party members holding union office in 1948. But he has not enquired how far these pronouncements and enactments affected the basic fabric of union institutions.

The TUC's files on the 1948 and 1949 statements show that the Organisation Department and the General Council chose *not* to wage an active anti-communist campaign, despite many appeals from trade union branches and trades councils to do so — including ETU branches anxious for assistance in combating corruption and CP influence. Despite Deakin's entrenched position, the awkward question remains unanswered of how Communists continued to be important in large swathes of the TGWU's life: for example, the London buses and Midlands' car factories. I think it likely that Deakin chose not to delve too deeply lest he find the many lay officials whom he had reason to suspect were CP members. The extent and the reasons for his and the Executive's acquiescence need investigation.

Trade unions' position in the National Dock Labour Scheme

The Labour government was committed to unions continuing their wartime position as co-partners in the economy. This role was expanded not only to the docks, but also in the newly nationalised industries. In the docks, private capital was not expropriated, merely controlled and circumscribed by the state. Nevertheless, under the National Dock Labour Scheme, the unions had a more visible and publicly legitimate role as co-partners in regulation than the 'consultation processes' of the nationalised industries.

A critical postwar feature emerges for the first time: unions accepting responsibility for helping to run a peacetime economy, for being a social partner. There was serious thinking going on about the dilemma and problems involved and how they could be resolved. In 1998, we are very badly served for scholarship which tells us what that thinking was and how the unions actually responded to the challenges. We are making do with mythology and conventional wisdom.

Phillips records Deakin's assessment of the National Dock Labour Scheme as worker control and agrees that the scheme provided for union officials' control of substantial aspects of dockers' employment. He quotes and concurs with other contemporary judgments that the TGWU's role was also compromising: its central part in the scheme's administration meant that it could no longer serve its members with undivided loyalty. However, having identified this major source of the three unofficial strikes he is analysing, he does not go on to consider either the actual measure of worker control in the scheme *or* how well or badly the TGWU responded to the challenge compared with other unions at the time faced with the same problems — the National Union of Mineworkers, the Railwaymen, ETU, etc.

Trade union activists and members in the late 1940s

Phillips states that the TGWU was out of touch with rank-and-file dock workers. But in contrast to the Labour Government's, Deakin's and many right-wing journalists' views, he does not view the influence of left-wing activists and Communists in particular as being important. He judges the unofficial dock strikes to be the normal response of ordinary dockers to grievances. Though it is clear that the strikes were precipitated by genuine grievances, Phillips does not prove his case. He fails to deal adequately with a number of cognate issues.

The 1945 dockers' charter

Phillips records that this was the result of an unofficial movement, but does not examine this movement's personnel or their behaviour. In fact, there was a rich vein of self educated socialist/syndicalist dockers who were in the van of unofficial leadership in London. Many may have been in the CPGB, but had been already politically formed before joining. Similar to the culture of the London busmen's rank-and-file movement, they form an important and un-researched background to the vicissitudes of docklands class conflict.

The 1949 Canadian seamen's strike

Phillips writes that dockers were motivated by 'the unofficial defence of a near-sacred dockland principle, the right to avoid blacklegging in a dispute between another group of workers...and their employers'. (p.104) He does not consider why this near-sacred principle was not operated in other disputes in the 1940s and 1950s, for example, during the many hard-fought unofficial strikes of British miners when American coal continued to be imported and unloaded.

Phillips evidently believes that the traditions of trade union activism were given, laid down on tablets of stone and spontaneously remembered and honoured. But this version of rank-and-file culture is contentious. I do not believe this was the case. It is clear that left-wing trade union activists were crucial in articulating, legitimating and enforcing the culture of union activism in the late 1940s. They were not coterminous with the rank-and-file, and they knew they were not, even though their rhetoric presented the illusory ideology: the rank-and-file movement equals the rank and file.

The Labour Government, the unions and union members

Phillips provides an abundance of important evidence here from Cabinet and departmental records. But he does not offer a critical analysis of the material. For example, it appears that Hartley Shawcross as Attorney General was responsible for the *mishandling* in 1951 of the Beckton gasstokers as well as the dockers. (Bevin had died the previous year and the government lacked his strong influence and sure hand in relation to industrial conflict.) Shawcross was a resolute and guileful cold warrior and from Phillips's evidence one feels that his motives in prosecuting under Order 1305 were highly disingenuous. But Phillips accepts them at face value. Minkin's rules for the great alliance were transgressed here and the episode deserves detailed attention.

I think that Phillips accepts too readily Hennessey's and Jeffrey's judgements about the proclamations of a state of emergency and the use of troops in unofficial dock strikes. They cite them as examples of the overbearing British state. But it is surely plausible that the state has a legitimate concern with seeing that its citizens were fed and warm. If the government's actions were unwarranted, why did the rank-and-file dockers not fraternise with the troops and deter them from strikebreaking? The dockers themselves apparently felt the troops were not transgressing on unspoken customary rules engagement in dock strikes. Phillips records the returns to work after radio broadcast appeals from Attlee and Isaacs during the unofficial dock strikes in 1945 and 1949, but offers no explanation of why they were successful. One plausible hypothesis is that dockers were moved by appeals from *their* government to consider the wider community. There are other possible interpretations which need articulating and then assessing.

We have many histories of the postwar Labour government's high politics, but very few detailed accounts of the period's social and economic history. *The Great Alliance* focuses on three crucial incidents of industrial conflict, and stimulates readers to ask the necessary awkward questions about the wider issues underlying them. Its timely publication will assist the painstaking scholarly work necessary to arrive at an overview of the rich, dense but problematic relationships between the government, the officials and activists inhabiting the edifices of the trade union movement and the working people who belonged to them and voted Labour

Nina Fishman
Nina Fishman has written extensively on the left and the trade union movement

Industrial democracy?

James Hinton, *Shop Floor Citizens: Engineering democracy in 1940s Britain* (Edward Elgar, Aldershot, 1994), ISBN 1-85898-081-X, £39.95

For a few years during the Second World War, workers in British war industry walked close to positions of influence in their workplaces, where they elected trade unionists to sit with managements on Joint Production Committees (JPCs), and in their industries where their representatives were involved in the planning machinery. These new functions trespassed upon the forbidden ground of 'managerial functions'. James Hinton's excellent book gives the first comprehensive account of what happened in the workshops and how, between 1941 and 1944, a framework of democratic planning, involving employers, unions (including shop stewards) and the state, evolved. He indicates that this might have become the instrument for realising the economic plans of the Attlee government. Instead bureaucratic and inadequate planning machinery gave way, by 1948, to Keynesian management of the economy from above. Hinton locates the root of this failure in the limited vision of the Labour government, 'which extended new social rights to the citizens, without attempting any equivalent transformation of the nature of political citizenship in Britain'.

Considerable weight is given to Communist thinking and policy on production from 1941, and the role of Communist shop-stewards in fostering a factory culture favourable to production is presented as 'an important factor in any reckoning of the potential for radical change in Britain during those years'. Every politically aware person who worked in engineering during the war knows this to be true, although it is one of the many truths buried by the Cold War. Any assessment of the role of the Communist party in the twentieth-century British labour movement must take Hinton's book into account, together with Nina Fishman's recent *The British Communist Party and the Trade Unions 1933–45*.

In 1939 much of British war industry was in a sorry state, with neither the machine tools nor the management ability necessary. Nor was there adequate state machinery to plan, organise and co-ordinate production. By 1941, in spite of heroic work in the wake of Dunkirk, there was an acute production crisis. Although government propaganda exhorted the workers to 'Give us the Tools and we will Finish the Job', and shook a finger at them with such inept slogans as, 'You Can't Spell Victory With an Absent T', there was widespread public perception that the fault lay with management. The phrase 'Blimps in the Boardroom' indicated this criticism of war production, and called for a direct route of co-operation between the workers and Whitehall...'craftsmen and statesmen must act as one' was hammered home by the Labour and Liberal press, especially by the *Daily Mirror*, a paper much read in the workshops. It was a line backed by a progressive minority of employers and managers.

While workers and managers blamed each other, both pointed a finger at Whitehall's weaknesses. There were three supply ministries (Aircraft Production, Admiralty and Ministry of Supply); their rivalries and divisions were damaging, and Bevin's Production Executive which was meant to co-ordinate them, had no powers. Even *The Times* and the *Telegraph* joined with the Communists in calling for a supreme Ministry of Production. This was not a demand for total centralisation of production. The Communist Party, for instance, called for such a ministry to act through the Regional Boards, which had been set up in 1940 as links between the Regional Officers of the supply ministries. The Boards should, the Communists argued, have a strong trade-union presence which would include representatives from the factories, and there should be direct access to the Boards from the shop floor. The Left saw this planning framework as one in which trade unionists, co-operating with progressive employers, could engage in the practicalities of administering the production drive. It was a vision shared by such employers, and especially by George Dickson, managing director of a Rochester engineering firm, and Norman Kipping, works manager of Standard Telephones and Cables in East London. Throughout the war and into the post-war years they continued to press their views in high places. Dickson pioneered the Capacity Clearing Centres, which spread from his firm in Rochester to cover the country. These provided a channel through which companies faced with bottlenecks could borrow temporarily unused tools and machines from other local firms, and could deal with problems of local labour supply, transport, and housing.

Such 'new broom ideas' did not altogether suit the supply ministries, which didn't want to be ordered about by a super ministry, or the Ministry of Labour, where Bevin was determined to preserve the voluntary character of collective bargaining, to keep wage bargaining and industrial relations out of the hands of the planners and to prevent the incorporation of the unions in the state machine. He thought that the credibility of trade-union leaders might be undermined if they became involved in the war economy and the revolutionary chaos of the First World War might be repeated. He seems to have overlooked the difference, that the shop stewards who led the 'revolutionary chaos' now had successors who were at the front of the production drive. Bevin also hated Beaverbrook, the chief candidate for the post of Supremo, while his political future, and that of Churchill, depended on keeping the balance between the parties in the Coalition. But, for the very reasons for which he opposed an all-powerful Ministry of Production, he supported regional devolution. What materialised therefore was a weak Ministry of Production, with tripartite Regional Boards.

The JPCs

The participation of workers in this process became real with the formation and spread of Joint Production Committees, on which representatives of 'both sides' sat and discussed the problems of the production drive in their own workplaces. These were mainly in engineering, but there was analogous machinery in the mines, and some other factories set up their own committees. For the formation of the JPCs the Communist Party was initially more responsible than anyone else. In the early part of the war trade unionism had developed rapidly in engineering. This was natural with declining unemployment, but also shop-stewards had busily recruited the new workers coming into expanding factories, and when the Emergency Works Order was made in 1940 used it to secure union recognition and enhance bargaining rights. When Germany invaded the Soviet Union in June 1941, stewards in some of the largest aircraft factories proposed joint committees where they could discuss joint production problems with managements.

An October meeting, held on Communist initiative at the Stoll Theatre in London, attracted a thousand stewards from factories all over Britain. They went back to their workplaces and began to negotiate the formation of JPCs. This was not always easy. The Engineering Employers' Federation (EEF) was totally opposed to any infringement of 'managerial functions', while some stewards saw the JPCs as a form of workers' control, and quickly antagonised their management. Many trade unionists, especially older ones, did not trust the Communists and were, anyway, unwilling to give up their hard-learned trade secrets to their managers. Perhaps for these reasons the campaign was more successful in the newly organised factories of the South and Midlands than in the old union fortresses of the North and Scotland.

What the Communist campaign did do was to convince the Government, the union leaders and the employers that it might be better for JPCs to become 'official', than to oppose them and so risk a further upsurge of Communist influence. (A parallel decision was taken that it would be better for the Establishment to lead the Aid for Russia Campaign than to leave it in Communist hands.) Union leaders saw danger in JPCs that were not part of 'official' union machinery or which included non-unionists. As a result a scheme was worked out by which all shop-floor workers elected their JPC representatives from among nominees of the unions, and Trade Union District Production Committees brought together the diverse unions in the engineering factories and kept an eye on the work of the JPCs. The obstinacy of the employers of the EEF was overcome when the unions signed an agreement with the Ministry of Supply to establish JPCs in all state-owned Royal Ordnance Factories. The EEF was then persuaded to 'strongly recommend' the establishment of JPCs in firms employing more than 150 workers. By April 1943 there were JPCs in some 75 per cent (2959) of larger firms and a further 1,606 in smaller ones. That JPCs were formed in the first place was because of Communist enthusiasm and organisation, but that the employers caved in was largely the work of Ernest Bevin, the Communists' arch-enemy.

James Hinton points out that what, in practice, JPCs achieved and how much they boosted production, is difficult to establish. There is a strong need for local studies to research what actually happened in individual factories. A 1943 survey showed that 70 per cent of engineering managements thought the committees had made a positive contribution to increasing efficiency and production. Their major contribution, he argues, was 'in creating a climate for greater trust and co-operation between management and workers'; but this was sometimes at the cost of a reaction from the shop-floor that the JPC had 'sold out' to management, especially where trade-union representatives became involved in disciplinary matters such as absenteeism, or where they failed to report back to their constituents. Frequently the union representatives were able to link health and safety, heating or canteen facilities to production, or to secure hairdressing or shopping facilities in the workplace. The AEU found that guaranteed piece rates and bonuses had been agreed in 40 per cent of establishments, so increasing the will to produce more. In a few cases inefficient managers were replaced as the result of union pressure.

Postwar aftermath

There were attempts, opposed by managements and not loved by union leaders, to link JPCs in an area, or in factories working on the same product. And there was pressure from most of the parties concerned, but opposed by the EEF, to tighten the links between JPCs, Regional Boards and Ministries. A democratic planning system might have emerged for the post-war economy. But it didn't. The Labour government had no such plans, even for nationalised industries. The TUC was content that its top leaders had access to the government and Whitehall. Employers' organisations were determined to make good the encroachments on 'managerial functions'. By the end of 1947 the Cold War had quenched Communist interest in the production drive. The Labour Left continued to advocate forms of industrial democracy but had little influence in industry. It was one of the great might-have-beens of history. I would argue that it was part of a wider historic failure.

The war saw the burgeoning of many forms of participative democracy and the flourishing of a democratic spirit in many areas of British society. The JPCs, with 20,000 trade unionists involved in their work in 1943, were only one manifestation. At a time of disillusionment in the ruling élites almost everywhere, ordinary people experienced the possibilities of democratic involvement in shelter committees, voluntary organisations, ARP, the

Home Guard, the flourishing culture of the 'People's War', even in the Forces. New concepts of citizenship were appearing. After 1945 these were aborted.

Perhaps, as James Hinton suggests of the defeat of the industrial democrats, defeat was inevitable. Very many, including some of the wartime activists, now wanted to 'put their feet up', especially as they had elected a government which, they hoped, would do all sorts of things for them. The dominant élites quickly set about reclaiming the territory they had lost. For the unions, voluntary collective bargaining was the Ark of the Covenant, although they went along with wages policy. But, when all is said, the Labour government must bear a responsibility for the failure. Its concept of democracy took no account of wartime developments, and it would not interfere with what Morrison, speaking of the House of Lords, called 'our old institutions' which in state and society frustrated any hope of a wider democracy.

But even if failure was natural in the circumstances, it is important to look at the potential which was created, especially now when socialists and democrats are discussing new ways forward. James Hinton's examination of what happened in industry is important and his concluding words are most apposite:

> It is precisely by listening to the clamour of voices drowned out by History's winners that we may be able to understand where our society went wrong and how it might yet reform itself.

Jim Fyrth
Jim Fyrth has edited Labour's High Noon *and* Culture and Society in Labour Britain

Class and politics

David James, *Class and Politics in a Northern Industrial Town: Keighley 1880–1914* (Keele University Press, Keele, Staffordshire, 1995) ISBN 1-85331-066-2, 224pp., £37.50 hbk

It would be very easy to criticise David James's book for its lack of depth and ideological direction, however, this would miss the point. This, his last book (David James died in July 1995) is aimed at a readership which has not yet come to be embroiled in the histographical nuances which colour

Labour History. Rather, James takes his readers by the hand and gently guides them through the basic tenets of Labour History's theoretical ruminations. This he tries to do in a simple but well-written introduction, in which he attempts to explain a number of different approaches to aspects of *'class'* its meaning and relationships to politics and society. Many may argue that James's approach is simplistic and somewhat naïve but there is a clear accessibility to the narrative and, through that, analytical thought. Thus the simple approach should be seen as a strength rather than a weakness. There is little point in immersing unsuspecting readers in the ideological boiling pot which is Labour History without first giving them a chance to understand a little about the different aspects of interpretation. Thus James's book is aimed at the general reader or first-year undergraduate, it is an introductory book, which he hopes will open wider vistas. For this reason it does not significantly add to the many debates which are ignited by terms such as *'class'* and *'politics'*. However it does build a platform which enables the reader to move on and progress to the theory-driven passions of a diverse number of labour historians all of whom are listed in a well-presented and informative set of notes at the end of each chapter as well as in a clear and easily navigated bibliography.

The thrust of James's book concerns the regional and local development of Labour representation in West Yorkshire, namely in the town of Keighley during the last twenty years of the nineteenth century and in the twentieth century before the First World War. He goes on to tie these events into the national picture, informing us, that while there have been a number of studies centred on northern industrial England none have specifically targeted Keighley. The importance of Keighley rests on its position as a leading industrial centre of the worsted wool trade and also in the fact that it developed labour organisations which remained vibrant and relatively well organised throughout the period in question. The leading labour organisation in this institutional development during the period of James's study is the ILP, and as such James hopes to fill a gap he believes has been left in understanding the growth and direction of the ILP, on both regional and national levels. James allows the reader to follow a well-defined narrative which builds on detailed local information and places the growth of labour generally and the ILP in particular within an ideological and cultural context. This context is strongest at the local level, as one would expect but it also takes in national and regional aspects. James goes on to paint a picture of the geographical and social influences as well as the economic which went to build the industrial community of Keighley and its surrounding district. When looking closely at the local nature of politics and society in Keighley it is clear James has a 'feel' for his subject. He also makes a point of being aware of different histographical ideas without stretching the patience of the reader, for example, comparing the situation in Keighley with those described by Patrick Joyce in the Lancashire cotton towns.[1] In this way James successfully explores the local and regional nature of the growing desire found for independent labour representation. By focussing on a locality such as Keighley, James shows that the nature of this desire was complex and had features which were unique to the district itself. However, he is able, in the style of the book, to make this complexity simple and accessible.

James looks at a number of different subject areas across a closely defined spectrum of class and politics. He attempts to assess the nature of working-class demands for representation and how and why these developed. He is clear that the main trend of the socialist desire in Keighley, if that indeed was what independent labour representation was all about, was of an ethical, reformist nature, rather than of a Marxian, revolutionary type, making clear that chief among the protagonists of this ethical socialism was Philip Snowden. James however, refrains from the temptation to write a book about Philip Snowden's early years; rather he places the spotlight on ethical socialism itself which allows the reader to get a 'feel' for the growth of labour organisation in the area and the ideological underpinning that went with it. Nevertheless, there is a weakness in this, the main section of the book. While James attempts to provide an account of the development of the local working class he is unable to provide a view for the majority of that same working class who were not involved in institutional organisations, be they the ILP or any other. There are accounts of the nature of Liberal and Conservative parties but these concentrate on the élites, such as the manufacturers and professional men who ran and financed those particular institutions; there is also a little about the social and church institutions which were financed by the same people. However, there is little for example about the majority of working men who voted for a Liberal MP throughout this period, there is also little said about the significant minority which voted Conservative, a minority which enabled the Conservatives to take control of the borough council after 1908. James also says very little about the formation of a branch of the SDF which lasted for just over a year in the late 1890s. All this would suggest then that the title of the book is a little misleading, we certainly do read about the class and politics of Keighley but only some of it.

The full impact of paternalistic influence is also somewhat glossed over. While there are many differences there also seem to be a number of similarities in Keighley with Patrick Joyce's Lancashire cotton towns.[2] Keighley after all is as near to some of the major cotton industrial centres as it is to Leeds and Bradford and had good transport links to Lancashire. Nevertheless, James makes the point that there are differences, the major one being economic and the effect the nature of the worsted trade and its profitability had on labour conditions and practice. The very fact that he feels the need to makes this point would suggest however that there were also similarities, something that James does not go into. However, in James's defence he does look into the relationship between the ethical socialists and local trade unionists, a relationship that threw up a number of ideological conflicts, potential splits and personal animosities and could be seen as a reflection of the national picture at the tail end of the nineteenth century. Thus, when we look at the book we are left with the economic and cultural arguments of the ethical socialist in the ILP set against the traditional liberalism of the manufacturers rather than a study of *class and politics*.

There seems to be little variation of this central theme and a great deal more might have been included if we were to understand the real meaning and relationship of terms such as class; therefore it is this limited comparison between ethical socialism and traditional Liberalism which forms the backbone of the book. Again, this is not a weakness as such when we consider the aim and range of the book. Rather in any 'study' of *class and politics* one would expect a greater depth, an expansion of the section on the influence of women for example, more on those who were to the left of the ethical socialists as well as those to the right. But then maybe, as I said at the beginning of this review, that would be to miss the point. David James has written a book that is a useful introduction to the influence of the industrial north of England on the development of labour representation which in itself is no mean feat.

Malcolm Starrs

1. P. Joyce, *Work, Society and Politics: The culture of the factory in late-Victorian England* (Brighton, 1980).
2. Ibid.

Rethinking Conservatism

John Charmley, *A History of Conservative Politics 1900–1996* (Macmillan, Basingstoke, 1996), viii and 283pp., ISBN 0-3335-6293-3, £16.99 hbk, and Brendan Evans and Andrew Taylor, *From Salisbury to Major: Continuity and change in Conservative politics* (Manchester University Press, Manchester, 1996), vii and 288pp., ISBN 0-7190-4291-7, £14.99 pbk

The Conservative Party used to be poorly served by historians and political scientists in comparison with the attention lavished upon the Labour Party. This neglect was odd since it is the Conservative party which has dominated government in the twentieth century, but in recent years it has begun to be rectified. These two books are part of a new wave of writing upon the party, its leaders, its policies, and its ideology. The main reason for the change is Margaret Thatcher's leadership of the Conservative Party between 1975 and 1990. To the dismay of Conservatives like Ian Gilmour she appeared to break many of the rules which had been responsible for the Conservatives' success in the past. Yet she led the party to three consecutive election victories. Trying to make sense of Thatcherism therefore invites a rethinking of the history of the Conservative party. Was it an aberration or a return to true Conservatism? What is the real identity of the party and the source of its success up to 1997?

These two books offer different reflections on the Conservative party in the twentieth century and the reasons for its success. Charmley has written an essay on Conservative leadership, which is lively, vituperative, exaggerated, but often shrewd portrait of each individual leader, sprinkled liberally with epigrams and anecdotes, and intemperate diatribes against liberals and psephologists. The performance is uneven, and there are surprising errors of fact; for instance, the Conservative slogan in 1959 was 'Life's better under the Conservatives: Don't let Labour ruin it', and 'Crisis? What Crisis?' was a *Sun* headline, not the words of James Callaghan as Charmley implies. There are numerous unsupported assertions and questionable judgements, but behind the brashness and the posturing there is a serious argument. Charmley is obviously rather proud of having been labelled a Thatcherite historian by one of the liberal newspapers he so despises. He is Thatcherite he tells us because he regards Margaret Thatcher as the greatest British leader this century, and it is from this perspective that he offers his account of Conservative leaders and the history of the party. He provides summary judgements, most of them unflattering, about past Conservative leaders. Balfour, Macmillan, and Heath come in for particular scorn, and Churchill does not escape censure, although he is surprisingly tolerant about Baldwin.

His heroine however is Margaret Thatcher. Her leadership knocked on the head the dominant liberal or Whig interpretation of Conservative history, which argued that the party has prospered by not being ideological but adapting to change by making concessions and compromises in order to maintain itself in government. Charmley does not dispute that this is how Conservatives often were able to hold on to office, but argues that it was at the expense of losing control of the political agenda. In some ways this is an old view of British politics. Parties of the left generate ideas for reform, but make a mess of implementing them, which is left to Conservative Governments to achieve in ways that do least violence to existing constitutional and institutional arrangements. Charmley argues that Thatcher exploded the myth that it was necessary for Conservative leaders to put survival in office above ideological principle. She reconnected the party to its core ideological principles — the protection of the nation and the protection of property rights. Under her leadership the Conservatives adapted to change by seizing the ideological initiative. They were not only electorally successful but also, for the first time this century, took control of the political agenda.

Perennial tension

Evans and Taylor have written a very different kind of book, drawing on a much wider range of sources and interpretations than Charmley. But like him they focus attention on why the Conservatives enjoyed such success and ascribe considerable importance to ideology. They argue their success can be explained by looking in detail at strategy, policy, and ideology in particular contexts. The tension between One Nation and neo-liberal ideology is not recent but perennial and takes different forms at different times. Methodologically both studies are primarily concerned with the Conservative party as the object of analysis, but whereas Charmley's focus is rather narrowly upon individual leaders, Evans and Taylor look more broadly at the Conservative party as an organisation, assessing the electoral and political strategy of the leadership as a whole, and the role played in different periods by ideological flexibility and organisational activism.

They do this extremely well for the earlier periods of the party's development, although their treatment of the Thatcher period through a review of different theories of Thatcherism sits rather oddly with the rest of the book.

The strengths of these studies is their recognition that ideology has been one of the crucial factors that has enabled the party to adapt to change, and maintain its pursuit of power. It has not been enough for the party just to be pragmatic. Their weakness is that they focus rather narrowly on one aspect of ideology, the role of the state in the economy. Charmley makes the important point that for the last hundred years the Conservatives have always been primarily an English party. It is their ability consistently to command a majority of English votes which has been the key factor in their success. Centre Left parties have had to rely on the votes of Scotland and Wales (and earlier Ireland) to get into office. Yet there is a paradox here.

The Conservatives have also been the champions of the Union, partly because the Union has been the vehicle of the wider British nationalism and sense of statehood which they were so keen to promote. The Union was intimately connected with the Empire, and the crumbling of the latter has been one of the factors in putting pressure on the former.

Charmley in particular does not seem to recognise this, arguing instead that the twentieth century has been dominated by a left-of-centre consensus on welfare and state intervention until the advent of Thatcher. But the real foundations of Conservative ideological dominance in the twentieth century lie in the Union, the Constitution, Property, and Empire. These are the key institutional and ideological pillars of the Conservative state and are the basis of the particular sense of national identity which the Conservatives have sought to defend.

They have suffered defeats — the House of Lords lost its veto, Ireland seceded and the Empire has gone — but it is remarkable how much of the old constitutional order has survived intact. This is the real heart of the ideological consensus and the secret of Conservative dominance of British politics. Concessions were made on welfare spending and union rights but although these modified basic property rights, at no stage did they fundamentally challenge them. The consensus Thatcher overthrew was therefore primarily over the role of the state in the economy, because she recognised (correctly) that it no longer needed to be sustained. But in many other areas she operated within the traditional consensus. She was a traditional Conservative in her efforts to conserve key features of the British state, particularly its role in the world, its constitution, and its unitary, centralised structure, against nationalist movements within the UK, and increasingly towards the end, her new enemy, the European Union. A full understanding of the role ideology plays in the Conservative party and the nature of English and British nationalism needs to consider these dimensions too.

Andrew Gamble

Andrew Gamble teaches at the University of Sheffield and is the author of numerous books and articles on twentieth-century economic and political developments

Books Received

Reviews of some of the following items are in preparation and will appear in future issues of the journal. Publishers sending items to be considered for review, and readers interested in reviewing any of the publications listed here, should write to Mike Waite, *Socialist History* reviews editor, c/o Burnley College, Higher Education Centre, School Lane, Burley, BB11 1UF.

Readers considering submitting articles other than reviews, or sending general correspondence, should write to the *Socialist History* editorial team c/o Willie Thompson, Glasgow Caledonian University, Dept of Social Sciences, Cowcaddens Road, Glasgow, G4 OBA.

Maggie Andrews, *The Acceptable Face of Feminism: the Women's Institute as a social movement* (Lawrence & Wishart, London, 1997), xv and 176pp., ISBN 0-8531-5833-9, £12.99 pbk.

Noreen Branson, *History of the Communist Party of Great Britain 1941–1951* (Lawrence & Wishart, London, 1997), viii and 262pp., ISBN 0-8531-5862-2, £1.99 pbk.

Brian Brivati and Tim Bale (eds), *New Labour in Power: Precedents and prospects*, (Routledge, London, 1997), xii and 212pp., ISBN 0-4151-7973-4, £12.99 pbk.

Laurence Brockliss and David Eastwood (eds), *A Union of Multiple Identities: The British Isles c.1750–c.1850* (Manchester University Press, Manchester, 1997), xviii and 222pp., ISBN 0-7190-5046-4, £40.00 hbk.

John Callaghan, *Great Power Complex: British imperialism, international crises and national decline 1914–51* (Pluto Press, Socialist History of Britain series, London, 1997), xiii and 144pp., ISBN 0-7453-1179-2, £9.99 pbk.

David Cesarani (ed.) *Genocide and Rescue: The Holocaust in Hungary 1944* (Berg, Oxford, 1997), vii and 220pp., ISBN 1-8597-3126-0, £1.99 pbk.

Phil Cohen, with a foreword by Gillian Slovo, *Children of the Revolution: Communist childhood in cold war Britain* (Lawrence & Wishart, London, 1997), 189pp., ISBN 0-8531-5841-X, £12.99 pbk.

Jack Dywien, *George Dimitrov: Fighter against Fascism* (Reprint of 1982 lecture published by the author, 22 Alexander Street, Nelson, Lancashire, BB9 8JF), 20pp., no ISBN, £1.00 pbk and postage and packing.

John Grayson, *Opening the Window: Revealing the hidden history of tenants organisations* (Tenant Participation Advisory Service, Manchester, 1996), 56pp., ISBN 1-8717-9650-4, £7.00 pbk (large format).

Dale T. McKinley, *The ANC and the Liberation Struggle: A critical political biography* (Pluto Press, London, 1997), ISBN 0-7453-1277-2, £11.99 pbk.

John Newsinger, *Dangerous Men: The SAS and popular culture* (Pluto Press, London, 1997), x and 160pp., ISBN 0-7453-1206-3, £10.99 pbk.

Geoffrey Ostergaard, *The Tradition of Workers Control* (Freedom Press, London, 1997), 160pp., ISBN 0-9003-8491-3, £6.95 pbk.

Keith Ansell Pearson, Benita Parry and Judith Squires (eds), *Cultural Readings of Imperialism: Edward Said and the gravity of history,* (Lawrence & Wishart, London, 1997), 304pp., ISBN 0-8531-5840-1, £14.99 pbk.

Morgan Philips Price, Tania Rose (eds), with a foreword by Eric Hobsbawm, *Dispatches from the Revolution: Russia 1916–18* (Pluto Press, London, 1997), xii and 181pp., ISBN 0-7453-1205-5, £8.99 pbk.

Robert Pope, *Building Jerusalem: Nonconformity, Labour and the social question in Wales, 1906–1939* (University of Wales Press, Cardiff, 1998), xiii and 269pp., ISBN 0-7083-141-3, £25.00 hbk.

Huw Richards, *The Bloody Circus: The Daily Herald and the left* (Pluto Press, London, 1997), x and 246pp., ISBN 0-7453-1118-0, £13.99 pbk.

Andrew Thorpe, *A History of the British Labour Party* (Macmillan, Basingstoke, 1997), xi and 300pp., ISBN 0-3335-6081-7, £12.99 pbk.

Correspondence

Dear Editor,

I am sorry that Max Morris feels I have been unfair to him in my book *The Death of Uncle Joe* (Merlin Press, £9.95), an extract from which was published in *Socialist History* No.10.

I do not dispute that Max Morris made his dissident views clear to John Gollan and other British Communist leaders. Any Communist could do this. Gollan always listened patiently. Not long after the Second World War, a soldier back from Berlin told Gollan what he had found out about the Russians. Gollan replied: 'I could tell you much worse things than that. But not outside this room.'

Comrades who accepted that restriction could indeed say what they liked, so long as it made no difference.

I admit that, at the beginning of 1956, we Party members all thought that this was the proper way for a Communist to behave. But, by the end of 1956, a great may of us had begun to see that this was the leaders' way of putting us in a cleft stick. If you talked to the capitalist press, you were a traitor. (Not until 1970 did it become apparent that we had all misunderstood this rule. It meant: 'You must not talk to the capitalist press unless you are Palme Dutt.') If you started your own paper, as the *Reasoner* comrades did, you were threatened with expulsion. If you kept quiet in public, you appeared before the world as a supporter of every wicked thing the Party and the Soviet Union did, because silence gives consent. It is not surprising that, by Easter 1957, about a quarter of the Party's membership had said; 'I don't want to play this game,' and walked out.

Those who stayed, like Max Morris, were accepting the principle of 'not outside this room'. If Max Morris can show me that he made any *public* protest about the expulsion of Peter Fryer from the Communist Party, the later expulsions of Brian Pearce and Hyman Levy or the imprisonment of Wolfgang Harich in East Germany, then I will gladly apologise. My recollection is that, whatever he said in private, he was silent in public. Does he still call this the behaviour of a disciplined comrade? I call it knuckling under.

Alison Macleod

Index

Abrahams, Ena 43
Acton, Lord 8
Adhikari, G. 29
Adler, Ruth, *A Family of Shopkeepers* 44
Admiralty, The 2, 3
Afghanistan 18
Aid for Russia Campaign 87
Aircraft production 86
Alexandria 11
Algeria 4, 19
Aliens Act (1905) 44, 45
Ancien Regime 77
Angell, Norman, *The Great Illusion* (1910) 11
Anglo-Persian war 1
Ankara 59
Ansell, Esther 45
Argentina 4, 66
Ataturk, Kemal 27
Austria 14, 73

Baldwin, Stanley (Prime Minister) 94
Bangladesh 33
Barclay, Tom, *Memoirs of a Bottlewasher* 48, 49, 50
Bengal 26, 28
Berlin Conference (1885) 7
Bernhardi, General von 11
Bevin, Ernest 86, 88
Boers 11, 12, 40
Borneo 1, 2
Brass, Paul 34
Brembre, Nicholas 63, 64

Brooke, James 1, 2
Brunei, Sultan of 1, 2
Burma 8, 10, 68

Caddick, Eric 55
Capacity Clearing Centres 86
Carpio, Salvador Caetano 68
Castaneda, Jorge 65
Castle, Cathy, *Britannia's Children* 39
Castro, Fidel 67, 68
Chartism 4, 75
Chaudhuri, Nirad C., *Thy Hand, Great Anarch* 28
Chile Solidarity Campaign 53
China 1, 3, 6, 20
Churchill, Winston (Prime Minister) 16, 87, 94
CIA 18, 67
Cochrane, Captain 2
Cold War 18, 61, 73, 89
Columbia 68
Communism 17, 70, 71
Communist party: of Great Britain 23, 30, 54, 86, 87, 88, 89; of Germany in exile 73
Conservative party 61, 92, 93, 95
Cross, Maire Fedelma 77
Cuba 67
Czechoslovakia 71, 73

Daily Mirror 86
Democratic Left 53
Derby, Earl of (Prime Minister) 2

Dickson, George 86
Durban 54, 56

East India Company 1, 2
East Timor 53
Eastern Europe 69, 70, 71
Edinburgh 5
Education Act (1870) 40
Egan, Terry 53
Egypt 8, 11, 12
El Salvador Sierra Maestra 68
Elgar, Sir Edward 40
Elgin, Lord (Viceroy of India) 3
Ellis, S. and Sechaba, T., *Comrades Against Apartheid* 53
Ellis, Sarah Stickney 77
Emergency Works Order (1940) 87
Empire Day 46
Engels, Friedrich 5, 6, 14
Engineering Employers' Federation (EEF) 87
Enterprise (Spaceship) 18
European Union 96

Fascism 65
Feltrinelli (Italian publisher) 65
Fenians 48
First World War 17, 38, 40, 49, 58, 76, 86, 90
Foreign Office 2
France: 7, 9, 13; French Resistance 19, 27; Revolution 4
Free German Youth (Great Britain) 72, 73
Freud, Sigmund 65

Galeano, Eduardo 69
Gandhi, M. 25, 28
German Democratic Republic 73
Germany 7, 9, 13, 17, 73, 74, 87
Gertler, Mark 43
Gilmour, Ian 93
Gladstone, William 11
Goebbels, Joseph 16

Gollan, John 54
Gott, Richard 65, 68
Grenada 18
Grocers' Company, London 63, 64
Guatemala 67, 68
Guevara, Ernesto 'Che' 65, 68, 69
Gulf War 18, 40

Halabja 58
Hamilton, Elizabeth 77
Havelock, Sir Henry 39
Heath, Edward (Prime Minister) 94
Hebrew School 49
Heine, Henrich 16
Heren, Louis 47
Hicks Beach, Sir Michael (Chancellor) 8
Hilferding, Rudolf 14
Hinden, Rita 61
Hindi 24, 32, 33, 34, 36
Hindustan Lever 34
Hinton, James 88, 89
History Workshop 37
Hitler, Adolf 16
Hobson, J.A. 12, 13, 14, 19
Home Guard 89
Honecker, Erich (Leader, GDR) 73
Hong Kong 20
Hylton, Lord 57

India: 32, 34, 35, 61; Arunachal Pradesh, 31; Communist Party of 29, 30; Emperor of 16, 20, 23; Gujarat 31; Jammu 35; Karnataka 31; Kashmir 35, 36; Kerala 28, 31; Lucknow 5; Maharashtra 31, 32, 33; Meghalaya 31; Mizoram 31; Mutiny 5; Nagaland 31; National Congress 25, 28; Northern State 32; Office 2; Rebellion 39; Tamilnandu 31
'Imperialism, Age of' 4
Ireland: 46, 95; Home Rule 11; Roman Catholics 47, 49 41, 43, 48
Istanbul 58, 59
Italy: Italians 7, 27; in London 42

James, David 90, 93
Japan 16, 20
Jews 47, 41, 42, 43, 46, 48, 51, 73
Jinnah, Muhammad Ali 29
Johnstone, Monty 29
Joint Production Committees 87
Jones, Creech 61
Joyce, Patrick 91, 92

Kashmir 35, 36
Kasrils, Ronnie (deputy Minister of Defence, South Africa) 54, 56
Kautsky, Karl 14
Keighley 90, 91, 92
Kerrigan, Rose 49
Khan, Hamje 32
Kipling, Rudyard 18
Kipping, Norman 86
Kirk, Neville 74
Korea 19, 20
Kristallnacht pogrom 73
Krupp 10
Kurdistan 57: Diyarbakir 57; Democracy Platform 57; New Year (Newroz) 57; Workers' Party (PKK) 57

Labour Monthly 29
Labour Party 61, 89, 93
Latin America 19, 65, 70
Leicester 48, 49, 50
Lenin, Vladimir Ilich 13, 23, 36
Liberal Party (Great Britain) 92
London: Bethnal Green 42; Clerkenwell 42, 49; Cockneys 47; Covent Garden 42; East End 50; Gore Road 48; Hackney 48, 49; Poplar 50; Sidney Street 49; Shadwell 47; Spitalfields 42, 43; Stepney 42
Luxemburg, Rosa 15
Lynch, Eric 53

Macmillan, Harold (Prime Minister) 94

Malaysia, 4, 7, 20, 31
Malmesbury, Lord (Foreign Secretary) 2
Marathas 34
Marx, Karl 5, 6, 13, 14, 23, 28, 36, 65, 91
Mental Defectives Act (1913) 41
Miaithili linguistic state 32
Ministry of Production 87
Mnacko, Ladislav 72
Museum of London 38
Muslims 24, 25, 26, 27, 28, 32, 33, 34, 35, 62, 68

National League 29, 30, 32
Nazis, Nazism 15, 17, 65
Nehru, P. 25, 28, 30, 36
New Zealand 5, 21, 37
Nicaragua 18, 53, 68
Northampton, John of 63, 64

O'Connor, Feargus 75
Opium Wars 1, 6
Ottoman Empire 27

Pakistan 18, 29, 30, 35, 36
Palme Dutt, R., *India Today* (1940) 24, 25, 29, 30
Panama 18
Panjab 31, 32, 33
Paraguay, Garaní speakers 21
Pender, Sir John 2
Pentagon 19
People's: Front 73; War 89
Perry, Commodore 1
Peru 7
Pilsudski 71
Polish Rebellion (1863) 5
Portugal 4
Postan, Professor Michael 13
Pridham, Geoffrey 70
Protestants 47, 48
Punjab 4

Ram Raj 26
Reform Act (1832) 12
Rhodes, Sir Cecil 11
Rice, the Hon. Charles Spencer 3
Richard II 63
Rome (Romans) 6, 17
Rushdie, Salman 18
Russell, Charles 51
Russell, Lord John (Whig Foreign Secretary) 3, 4
Russia 5, 7, 9, 45

Sabah (British North Borneo) 4
Saigon 1
Salisbury, Lord 9
Sandhurst 26
Sarawak (Sarahwa) 1, 9
Saussure, Albertine Necker de 77
Schopenhauer 11
Sea Dayaks 1
Second World War 17, 29, 60, 72, 74
Shivaji 33
Sikhs 33, 34, 35, 47
Singapore 20
Snowden, Philip 91
Social Democrats 14
Solomons, Yetta 45
Somalia 55
South Africa 53, 54, 55, 56
South Korea 19
Southgate, Walter 48
Soviet Occupation Zone 73
Soviet Union 71, 87
Spain 1, 4, 5, 73
Spanish Civil War 52
Spencer, Herbert 7
Spice Islands 2
Spitalfields 42
Sriramalu, Potti 31
St John, Spenser 2
St Patrick's Day 47
Stalin, Joseph 9, 16, 24, 29

Standard Telephones and Cables 86
Stock Exchange 14
Sudan 8, 9
Supply, Ministry of 86

Tailors' Fraternity of St John the Baptist 64
Tamils 34
Tandon, Prakash 34
Telegu 31; speaking 34
Thailand (Siam) 9
Thatcher, Margaret (Prime Minister) 93, 94, 95
Thew, Angela 53
Toynbee Hall 51
Trade Union District Production Committees 88
Transkei, East London 55
Tristan, Flora 77
Turkey 13, 27, 58

United States of America 5, 10, 13, 17, 18, 20, 21, 31, 35, 60, 67, 74, 75, 76
Urdu 34
Uttar Pradesh 26

Vanhanen 70
Victoria, Queen 9, 41

Walesa, President Lech 71
Waller, Michael 71
Weinreicht, Max 34
Wellington, Duke of 46
West Indies 47, 51
William II 10, 15

Yiddish 44, 45, 47

Zangwill, Israel, *Children of the Ghetto* 45, 50, 51, 52

Titles of Related Interest

Growing Up Poor
Home, school and street in London 1870–1914
Anna Davin

> 'A wealth of oral history archive material...covering the era of Victorian social reform from the workhouse to the beginnings of the welfare state....The memories of those who grew up poor, the writings of social reformers, educationalists, local records and reports give life to the history of social change.' *Socialist Review*

Awarded 1996 *History Today*/Longman History Book of the Year Special Prize. Chosen as 'best of tomes' by Claire Tomalin, *Guardian*
A *History Guild Book Club* selection

A founding member of the History Workshop, Anna Davin is an editor of *History Workshop Journal*. She teaches at the University of Middlesex and has been a visiting lecturer at Binghamton University, SUNY since 1979.
ISBN 1 85489 062 X (hb) £19.95
ISBN 1 85489 063 8 (pb) £12.95

Masters and Servants
Class and patronage in the making of a labour organisation
Huw Beynon and Terry Austrin

> 'Handsomely presented....Immensely rich, an impressive body of material on the historical analysis of trade unionism...For those interested in social history, politics, and sociology, this is a very important book whose richness and originality make it an indispensable work.'
> *Sociological Review*

This book offers a detailed understanding of mining society, trade unionism, and the public and private lives within communities. Speaking through contemporary reports and the authors' interviews, people are at the heart of this account.

Huw Beynon's books include *Working for Ford* and the award-winning *Digging Deeper*. Terry Austrin is at the University of Canterbury.
ISBN 1 85489 001 8 (hb) £21.95
ISBN 1 85489 000 X (pb) £12.95

SUBSCRIBE TO SOCIALIST HISTORY

Annual subscription for individuals is £15 waged, £10 unwaged and £25 to overseas members. Send subscription with name and address to:
>Secretary,
>Socialist History Society,
>6 Cynthia Street,
>London N1 9JF

Institutional and library subscription is £25 per annum. Send requests to:
>Subscriptions,
>Rivers Oram Press,
>144 Hemingford Road,
>London N1 1DE